# PROPERTY LADDER
hints&tips

# PROPERTY LADDER
## hints&tips

SARAH BEENY
with Barty Phillips

CASSELL ILLUSTRATED

First published in Great Britain in 2006 by
Cassell Illustrated,
2–4 Heron Quays, London E14 4JP
a division of Octopus Publishing Group Limited

Text by Sarah Beeny with Barty Phillips

Editorial, design and layout by
Essential Works,
168a Camden Street, London NW1 9PT

A CIP catalogue record for this book is available
from the British Library.

ISBN-13: 978-1-844035-18-2

ISBN-10: 1-844035-18-2

Printed in China

Information compiled from *Property Ladder:
The Developer's Bible* (Cassell Illustrated)

# Contents

# Introduction

Every time I have a question about anything I ring my father – who either knows the answer or just happens to have a book to hand with the answer. The great thing is that his answers are concise and clear and if not you can always ask again. For those of you not fortunate enough to have his phone number, you have this handy book! It contains clear, easy to understand information on all aspects of buying a property.

It is now about four years since *Property Ladder* the series first started. Much has changed since then. The property market itself has fluctuated, although actually remained relatively stable, while our television screens are now full of variations on the theme, some more interesting than others.

During these last few years, there has clearly been no decline in the nation's interest in buildings. Since our cave days, we have wanted our surroundings to be not only comfortable but also aesthetically pleasing. So, it is not surprising that there is a demand for our homes to evolve in both ways.

The design of a house is therefore about both these important issues. A perfect home must be lovely not only to look at but also to live in, and our diverse population ensures many variations on these ideals. I am endlessly impressed by people's willingness to stamp their personal mark on their homes. From the monastically minimalist to the wild and wacky, the time and effort devoted is admirable.

Does all this home-creating make us happier? That I am not sure about. Most psychologists agree that our surroundings contribute to our contentment. As long as it is not to the detriment of interest in the general community, this inward contentment can only be a good thing. If we can be depressed by lack of light, we can be so by lack of design.

Whilst we all may want to create our own very special home, most people don't actually want to live in a building site or do building work, so a newly developed house provides the perfect blank canvas for someone to create their own home environment. There is therefore a demand for newly modernised homes, where all the hard work has already been done, and that is where a developer's market is.

New development also ensures the creation of a house suited to today's lifestyle. What was practical years ago may no longer be so, as the galley kitchen shows. The days when whoever was cooking would disappear and busy themselves are gone. Our hectic lives – often with all adults working – means that time spent at home needs to be with friends and family, so the kitchen/breakfast/living room is now better suited to the way we live. In time, no doubt, things will change again, but for now big, flexible space is the order of the day.

Decorative ideas date more quickly, as they do not require our lifestyles to evolve in order to change. It is here that most people can indulge themselves with a bit of creative flair in their own homes. My advice is don't abandon a decorative concept halfway through or it is unlikely to work. Once you have the initial idea, go ahead, dare yourself to carry it off – unless, of course, the house is a development project, in which case keep it simple, make the house work perfectly for your market and let the new purchaser turn it into their home.

# 1 property development

Developing a property means altering it from the state it's in to a more marketable state and, for your efforts, making a profit in the process. This may sound simple but throughout the project, from purchase to final sale, a whole range of skills will be necessary. Even experienced developers find that property development can be stressful, expensive, time-consuming and fraught with crises. For the beginner, taking on the first project can be a high-risk business.

# A businesslike approach

Firstly, start thinking like a developer. It is important to bear in mind that you are running a business, not buying a home for yourself. Don't think of the property as 'yours'. It's a business proposition and, as with any business, if you do not make a profit then there will be no money to develop another property and therefore you have no business.

One thing is for certain, though. If you don't actually enjoy the process of buying, developing and selling, you are unlikely to succeed. However, you must also get each part of that process right if you want to stand any chance of making a profit.

Your property is simply a product. Develop it for a particular market and be objective – it's not going to be yours in the long run. Keep in mind your end product. Create a realistic budget and stick to it.

Don't be tempted to make expensive, unnecessary changes that won't add to its final value.

## Be organised

Buy a filing system, a concertina pocket system or box files. Keep records of everything you have researched, everyone you have contacted and their quotes. These records can be invaluable to refer to for future developments. Make sure you keep a clear set of accounts for yourself and for your accountant.

## Do your sums

Do your research and find out whether the property you are interested in can actually make you money. Be realistic about the costs of all the works and also set aside a contingency sum. Modernising an older building is an uncertain business and problems will arise along the way. Do not delude yourself into thinking that just because a property requires modernisation there is profit in modernising it.

## Get professional advice

Ask the experts. They have training and experience and their advice can prevent you from making expensive and time-consuming mistakes. From the initial purchase to the planning and developing, professional advice can be invaluable.

## Be realistic

Unless you are very experienced in general building work, it may end up being more expensive to try and do the work yourself than to pay an experienced workforce to do it for you.

## Thinking it through

Have you thought about why you are considering such an undertaking. Before you make the decision to go ahead and buy a property for development, check that you are doing this for the right reasons. It is imperative that you think it through to make sure you can cope with the financial, organisational, design and labour aspects before you begin.

CHECK**LIST** FOR BUDDING DEVELOPERS

*Ask yourself the following questions and if the answers are not favourable, make sure you can afford to buy in the necessary skills.*

1   *Have you or can you obtain enough money for: a) the initial purchase; b) the purchase and legal fees, and borrowing costs; c) specialist advice and help; d) building materials; e) the building work; f) furniture if dressing; g) contingencies (things that go wrong or for the unexpected).*

2   *Are you objective enough to develop the property for the most likely buyers and not as a self-indulgence to fulfil a dream of your own?*

3   *Are you prepared/experienced enough to do some of the work yourself?*

4   *Are you hoping to use friends to help with the work? Are you sure you are not stretching your friendship a bit far by asking them to do the work for free? (By accepting a favour you have little control over timescale or quality of work.)*

5   *Are you intending to manage the project yourself. If so, have you the skills required to do such work? Can you juggle the tradesmen, ordering of materials, and the order of work? Do you have a contingency plan for your contractors if you have to wait for planning permission or other delays?*

6   *Have you an understanding of basic building practices and interior spaces? Can you design a satisfactory workable plan, if you and the property require it, and do you know where to find a designer or an architect if you need one?*

7   *Have you a lot of patience, an ability to manage a workforce and a proper businesslike attitude to the whole project?*

8   *Have you explored the market?*

# Buying to sell

The most important thing when buying to sell is to keep the image of your target market in your mind at all times. Be sure to work out your figures after viewing any property you are serious about.

The most simple and comprehensive way to work out the maths is to subtract the associated fees and costs, renovation and purchase costs from the potential selling price of your property.
To get to this stage, calculate the following:
- The realistic resale value of the property.
- The cost of renovation works to the property.
- The sum total of all associated fees and costs you will incur during the project.

## The realistic resale value

Ask yourself what your property will be worth in peak condition. Finding out the realistic resale value or 'ceiling price' of a property can tell you instantly whether you have a deal. It will guide you towards buying for the right price, reveal how much the property will be worth once it looks its best and help you work out your potential profit margin. So, before investing in a property, ensure that calculating its realistic resale value is your prime concern.

- Build a profile of the property. Be realistic and base your profile on the location, building type, number of rooms, features and layout.
- Next, contact three local estate agents. Ask how much newly modernised properties of this profile have recently sold for in your area. See how the details of these properties match your profile.
- Calculate a resale value from the comparables that match your profile. If the sale of a comparable property took place more than two months ago, get an up-to-date opinion of the resale value of a similar newly renovated property. Then get two more estimates to substantiate the first.

## Administrative costs

Once you have worked out your realistic resale value, look at the administrative costs and budget. Buying a property always costs more than the purchase price. You will need to include the following costs in your calculations: legal fees (solicitor's/conveyancer's fees); stamp duty (a government tax on properties over £60,000); borrowing set-up costs and interest. Your lender will want to carry out a valuation (around £150) on the property to check that their loan is secure.

There are also extra fees such as the cost of the survey; Land Registry costs; site services – gas, water, electricity and council tax. Don't forget to include other administrative costs specific to your project, for example, the costs of selling the property once developed, planning and building control fees.

## Living in your development

If you are short of cash, and are generally pretty hardy, you could certainly consider living in your development. This may sound like a simple option but it does have its pitfalls.For example, are you really going to be able to continue to live in the property while the work is being carried out? This can be noisy, dusty, and intrusive and you may find yourself without facilities such as hot (or cold) water, use of a loo or a basic kitchen while the work is in progress, and this situation could last for weeks.

*As with all developments you want to be very sure that the work you do is actually going to raise the value of the property.*

It is vital to do your research first. Don't assume that if you do what you want this will automatically increase the value of the property. Even if you were to convert the loft or add an extension, you might find that the costs involved would exceed the amount that it adds in value to the property.

# Buying to let

Rather than sell a property, many people choose to buy one, develop it and then let it out, hoping that their capital asset will increase while they receive a stable income over a number of years. During the late 1990s residential property investment became increasingly popular as property prices rose, interest rates fell and specialist buy-to-let mortgages were created. At the same time the stock market became lacklustre and other forms of long-term investment failed to recover from the scandals of the time.

The popularity of buying to let increased rapidly and this helped to fuel the increase in property prices by an average of 15% in 2001, while the stock market fell by more than 15% in the same period. Many sectors of the general public lost confidence in investing in stocks and shares and even more people were compelled to buy to let.

## The future

At the time of writing growth in the rental sector is anticipated to continue because:

- Some potential buyers are being cautious and choosing to rent rather than buy or sell, while they wait for the property market to stabilise.
- First-time buyers are waiting longer before buying property. Many young people still decide to move out of their family home and the only affordable way to do this is by renting.
- The increasing number of company relocations away from the South-East is creating new demand for rental properties. Also, the majority of workers on short- to medium-term contracts, and those on contract from overseas, will rent.

In short, the strength of the rental market seems set to continue. However, there are great swathes of the UK where an excess of housing stock to let has driven rents downwards – most notably in major cities and especially at the cheaper end of the housing market.

1   Carry out thorough research. Check local rental conditions, analyse rental demand and determine the types of renting in your area. Look for clues such as a large company relocation, the opening of trendy bars and shops (for young professionals) or the existence of good schools (for families) and choose a property that will appeal to your market.

2   An appealing rental property is one that is close to transport links and/or has off-street parking.

3   If you plan to rent your property to professionals, all of the bedrooms should ideally be doubles.

4   Think low maintenance. You want a property that will run itself as smoothly as possible.

5   If you are managing the property yourself, be prepared to do some hard work.

6   Choose a property close to home that will enable you to sort out any problems easily.

7   Bear in mind that family rental homes require plenty of space and storage.

8   If you are the sole freeholder of the property, you will need to ensure that the common parts and the exterior of the property are well maintained. If your buy-to-let is leasehold, the responsibility for the maintenance of the exterior and interior communal areas will rest with the freeholder unless your lease specifies otherwise.

9   Steer clear of large gardens, unless you intend adding the cost of a gardener to the rental.

10  Consider whether you want to let furnished or unfurnished. Sometimes there is little difference between rents for unfurnished compared with part-or fully furnished properties. It all depends on your market and the demand in your area. Before looking for furniture, do your research.

## Buy to let as pension or investment

When rental returns are not booming you are likely to have to hang on to your rental property for at least ten years if you want to make money. Even then, after all the hard work and stress of renting a property, there is still no guarantee that your asset will increase in value. Consider the following:

- The state of the market and predicted conditions
- Interest rates have a direct impact on prices – any changes will affect the stability of the market.
- See how buying to let compares with other forms of long-term investments. Note that you will have to pay tax if your capital appreciates in value.

## Financing a buy-to-let

The general characteristics of a buy-to-let mortgage are as follows:

- Mostly available for between five and 45 years and for up to 80% of the property's value.
- Your income will be taken into account by the lender and you will be able to make before-tax deductions against the rental income for costs such as insurance, maintenance and agents' fees.
- You can claim for replacing items of furniture, fittings or fixtures, although their original costs are not tax deductible. Alternatively, you may find that a 'wear and tear' allowance based on 10% of your rental income is deductible.
- Insurance cover is available for the buildings and contents, as well as legal expenses in the event of court action against a defaulting tenant.
- Many lenders expect landlords to use a letting agent to manage the property and for an Assured Shorthold Tenancy Agreement to be drawn up.

**Additional costs**  For most investments lenders require that your gross return (the total rent received before tax) is at least between 130% and 150% of your monthly mortgage repayment. This helps budget for the additional financial commitments required when buying to let, which many investors often underestimate.

# Letting to buy

In the 1990s, when interest rates were low but the housing market slowed due to oversupply, many home-owners found that they were unable to sell their properties for the amount they wanted to so decided to let to buy. Rents were high and home-owners could not afford to buy a second home. Many decided to let their homes and buy another property to reduce their outgoings. If you let your own home to pay for a second property to develop, be realistic about the rental market in your area.

**Current economic climate** Today, letting to buy is still popular. Rather than selling a home to fund a new purchase, some home-owners are taking advantage of the low interest rates and, in theory, improving their pension prospects by renting out a property they no longer want to live in, in order to cover a second mortgage. Others are choosing to rent out a property rather than sell it due to the perceived instability of the property market.

If you really want to sell you have to be realistic about the asking price. Letting to buy sounds like a good prospect in today's climate but think hard before you rush into anything.

*It works best with an average priced property; you may struggle to get enough rent to pay a mortgage on an expensive home.*

## Money from lodgers

If neither buying to let nor letting to buy seems a viable option for you, you can always consider renting out a room in your own home to accrue extra income from your property. This is especially useful and least stressful if you rent for a relatively short period of time so as to fund your next property purchase.

# Assessing your skills

Think your project through and assess your own skills for dealing with each stage. Where you do not possess the necessary skills, set money aside for getting the professionals in to do the job.

## The purchase

Are you confident you can assess the housing in the area you've chosen? If not, get advice from local estate agents and your surveyor. Before you buy find out about the condition of the property and the market. If you are planning on buying at auction you need to do all this research before the auction date.

## The money

Do you know where and how you are going to borrow the money for the purchase price, legal and professional fees, loan costs, insurance costs and all the other things you will need to pay for, quite apart from the cost of the actual building work?

## The budget

Underestimating the cost of the development is one of the most common errors. You need to work out an accurate total budget and work within it. There are nearly always hidden costs so make sure you have a healthy contingency fund.

Be realistic about the work required, don't brush any costs under the carpet. Don't forget time delays also cost money. Simply waiting for six weeks for planning permission or delivery of materials or fittings that have not been ordered in time can add to the cost in terms of extra loan repayment. If in doubt, ensure you get professional estimates done.

## The plan

Even if it's just a question of redecorating, unless you are a confident designer it is nearly always best to get a professional architect or designer to have a look at the possibilities (and impossibilities) for the property. When it's a question of carrying out major works such as knocking down walls, building extensions, doing loft or cellar conversions, an inexperienced developer can come unstuck very quickly. With initial advice from an architect or designer, you will be able to get a good idea of what you can and cannot do, with or without official permission, and if you do need to get permission what is likely to be acceptable.

There may be by-laws and legal restrictions on the work you can undertake and it can be helpful to consult someone who knows the ropes. They will be able to advise you on the best use of space.

## ☑ CHECK**LIST** FOR DEVELOPERS

1   *Decide whether you want to buy to sell or buy to let. Each requires a different approach and you need to be sure which one you have chosen.*

2   *If you decide that the only way you can get going is by letting to buy, check on the current letting situation and that you will receive enough money to cope with the mortgage and the costs of developing.*

3   *Make sure your budget for any renovation or conversion work is realistic and allow enough for the inevitable contingencies.*

4   *Assess your skills realistically and be prepared to buy in any skills you don't have.*

5   *Make sure the work is well finished. If you skimp on the details it will put a lot of potential purchasers off.*

6   *Ensure that you get your priorities right. Check that the fabric of the building is sound before embarking on expensive alterations.*

# Money matters

Part of your original planning must include how you will finance your purchase and any building works. If you are a first-time buyer finding a suitable property and financing the purchase may seem like an impossible task. Even if you have owned a property previously but are looking for another, trying to work out what all the available options are can be as stressful as doing it first time around. But take heart. If hundreds of thousands of households in England can do it, so can you.

> *The idea of legal documents, large sums of cash and all the red tape that inevitably surrounds anything to do with property ownership may seem very daunting.*

## The process

The finances you have available will influence every aspect of your project, from which areas and type of housing you can consider to whether you will buy to let or buy to sell. Cash-flow will determine how quickly you can realise your plans and managing cash-flow successfully is part of the skill of being a successful developer. Every aspect of the process of property development relies on you being a successful property manager. The process involves:

- Conducting initial research on areas, property types and finance options.
- Finding a suitable property.
- Arranging your finance.
- Getting a survey.
- Working out your budget.
- Finding contractors/sub-contractors.
- Getting quotes.
- Finding and getting professional advice.
- Managing the project and finances.
- Managing your profit and taxes.

# Finding the money

When you have an idea of the sort of property you feel able to take on, you must then make sure you can finance the project. The general rule is that you can relatively easily secure a mortgage of at least up to three-and-a-half times your annual income and up to 70% of the value of the property.

**First-time buyers** There are three ways for first-time buyers to get onto the property ladder without too much difficulty. These are to find the right mortgage for the particular property you have in mind or choose a smaller property; to split the cost of the mortgage with another party – say a friend or partner or a member of your family; or to apply for a government or council scheme.

There are a confusing number of mortgage options available. Mortgage companies can make their offers sound much more generous than they actually are and may well imply your income can cope with higher payments than it actually can.

## Mortgage advice

- Take time to study the whole business of mortgages and borrowing money.
- Make sure you understand the technical terms and are aware of the implications that each deal could have for you if interest rates rise, for example.
- Approach several different mortgage lenders, or an independent mortgage broker, to see what loans and what types of mortgage are available.
- Don't jump at the first deal you are offered and don't be tempted to stretch yourself too far.
- Once you have decided on your lender, ask for a written 'offer in principle' to confirm the terms.
- Wise developers will buy at a price that assures them a 20% gross return of their total investment. Though you may develop with a slightly lower percentage profit rate, err on the side of caution.

# Finding the right mortgage

In recent years interest rates in the UK have been at their lowest for 30 years and although they have risen slightly are still a competitive business for lenders. In general there are two types of mortgages: interest-only and repayment mortgages, with variants of both on the market.

**Interest-only mortgages**  With an interest-only mortgage your monthly payments will only cover the interest on the loan taken out. The full amount borrowed needs to be repaid by the end of the loan term. Most people with an interest-only mortgage invest additional money each month into a savings fund with the expectation that it will grow at least enough to enable them to repay the loan at the end of the term. An endowment is one of these means of saving. Your lender may also insist on life insurance to cover the repayment of the loan in the unlikely event of you dying before the mortgage is paid off.

**Repayment mortgages**  With a repayment mortgage your monthly payments repay some of the capital along with the interest on the loan. No other way of repaying the mortgage is needed although, as with interest-only mortgages, your lender may also insist on life insurance in case you die.

# Buying jointly

If you prefer not to work alone or cannot afford to invest in a property on your own, you might consider buying jointly. Getting a joint mortgage will increase your borrowing power. Theoretically you can apply for a joint mortgage for up to four people although most lenders base their calculations for a loan on the incomes of two people. As with a single borrower, the amount is generally based on three-and-a-half times the main income, but with a second borrower add one of the secondary incomes to the equation.

Just remember, though, that whilst more people in your new enterprise can provide the comfort of more brains to tackle problems, not to mention more money, the more people in the equation the more difficult it can be to reach decisions.

**Other ways of splitting the cost**  A parent or family member may be willing to act as guarantor on your loan. If so, it is important that all parties fully appreciate the implications of this arrangement – that the guarantor becomes liable for the loan in its entirety should your payments fall behind.

**Contractual agreement**  If you do buy with a partner (or partners) you must have an agreement drawn up by a solicitor. This should state how much each party is contributing in terms of the down-payment and who is going to be responsible for the mortgage repayments (though legally you are jointly and severally liable). It will also state what percentage of the profit is to belong to each of the parties, and the course of action to be taken if one owner wishes to sell the property early. Such an agreement will make things clear from the beginning and hopefully avoid a disagreement from occurring.

---

**KEYPOINTS** FOR JOINT PURCHASE

*If you are buying jointly, do the following:*

***Spend time*** *discussing how the partnership will work.*

***Make sure*** *your solicitor draws up a contract between you, even if you are sure you will never fall out.*

***Decide*** *between yourselves who will be responsible for what aspects of the project and exactly what your plans are for your development.*

***Don't*** *leave anything to chance – it's easy to assume you are both thinking along the same lines and then find out later that you each have something quite different in mind for your development.*

***Make sure*** *you set aside an official time weekly to discuss any issues either of you are concerned about.*

# Create and control a budget

One of the most common and most serious mistakes made by first-time developers is to underestimate the budget. Make up your mind what you are doing and if you really are property developing then that is a business. You must include all your outgoings and costings, allow for contingencies and know where you can make cutbacks if the budget looks like it is getting out of hand. Burying your head in the sand and not looking at the sums because you don't like what you see is not fooling anyone but yourself. An overspend will not go away and managing the money does require organisation and discipline. Don't forget if there is no real profit at the end of the year your business will not be able to trade.

*It is absolutely vital to work out a realistic budget, and to make sure the amount you buy your property for makes it a sound investment.*

## Cash flow

Remember, cash flow is the key to success or failure. Plan your budget meticulously and itemise in detail the things you will have to pay for. You will find that you end up drawing on the money by degrees. Avoid getting carried away at the beginning of a project just because your bank balance is looking healthier than it has done in years – you may find that there is nothing left for crucial works later on, leaving you with no alternative but to cut corners to get the work finished. Working out a realistic budget in the first place is the answer to this. It is absolutely vital to make sure the amount you buy your property for makes it a sound investment before you commit yourself; rather than buying something that happens to be unmodernised and then discovering that the cost of the development and the purchase price actually adds up to more than you can sell it for.

## How much will it cost?

If you itemise realistically you can work out a sound allocation of costs. The maths may seem a bit overwhelming and the probable costs may seem terrifying but if you are not realistic at this stage you will be in for big trouble later on. The most common expense to overlook is the actual cost of buying, owning and selling the property. You also need to include everything from major repairs and structural alterations to light fittings and bathroom and kitchen fixtures. Most importantly, don't forget to factor in the cost of labour.

**Schedule of the works**  Experience will help you know how much something is likely to cost, but before you have built up the experience it is useful to make a detailed schedule of the works that need to be carried out on the property, with drawings if necessary. Then approach builders and collect together your quotes. Go over this budget over and over again and adjust it as necessary. If you have no experience of what these costs are and are not used to working out a budget, it is easy to miss vital items, forgetting to include, say, stamp duty or perhaps even the wiring, and especially forgetting that there will certainly be unexpected expenses on the way.

## Mortgage protection

Remember that if you decide to give up your job or are made redundant during your development project or if you become ill or injured, you may have difficulty keeping up your mortgage payments. You cannot rely on the State to help to cover the payments. There is no help for the first nine months of unemployment or disability for mortgages. It may be worth buying extra cover to protect your mortgage payments in case this situation arises. Policies differ, so always check them very carefully

*Don't be tempted to spend money on things just because you like them. Make your money matter – spend where required but not where desired. Other guidelines include:*

**Get a survey done** *before you purchase any property, make sure you understand its problems, know what work is needed and whether this is the project for you.*

**Get a second opinion** *and check what has been sold for what price recently, and ask the estate agent you are planning to sell the property through what they think will add value to the property.*

**Be aware** *of current Building Regulation requirements and adhere to them. Seek advice from the Building Regulations Officer at your local council planning department. Most planning departments are very helpful, so ask their advice.*

**Have integrity** *in your product – do a job properly or not at all. Purchasers and certainly their surveyors are not foolish and so don't labour under the illusion that you won't get found out.*

**Design for your market** *and not for yourself. While keeping the décor as neutral as possible, don't feel that you have to make the property bland. Create the best possible layout but leave scope for potential buyers not to feel smothered by your design.*

**Don't forget** *that to succeed and to make a profit you must be businesslike from start to finish.*

**Adopt an organised approach** *to the venture, getting advice where it is needed, keeping efficient records and doing things methodically. Then if things go wrong, you have your files and records to refer to.*

**Make lists** *and don't rely on your memory.*

**Deal with** *all potential difficulties before they reach a head.*

# The tax situation

Once you have made a profit from any development and sale you will have to consider tax.

## Principal Private Residence Relief

If the house is your only home and your place of residence, then you are allowed to sell it on and keep the profit and not pay any tax at all.

## Capital Gains Tax (CGT)

If the property is not your place of residence you are liable to pay this tax, although as an individual you are allowed to make capital gain a percentage of the profits before you are liable to pay CGT. Any gain above this limit is charged at different rates depending on your circumstances (although not more than the top rate of 40%).

## Income Tax

A professional property developer has to pay income tax on the profits. Help sheets are available free from the Inland Revenue website. Developers with queries regarding the allowability of expenses are advised to seek the advice of their local Tax Office as all cases are different.

## VAT

VAT is a tax chargeable on taxable supplies made in the UK by 'taxable persons'. All types of supply of goods or services (outputs) are covered by VAT law, whether of a revenue or capital nature. Supplies include the sale, hire or loan of goods. Outputs usually fall into one of four categories:

- Positive rated: taxable at 17.5% or at a rate of 5% for some supplies including construction work on property conversions, domestic fuel and power and energy-saving materials.
- Zero-rated: including 'socially or economically important' items e.g. public transport, children's clothing and so on.

- Exempt supplies including 'necessities' e.g. most forms of insurance, postage, finance and so on.
- Other: some supplies are outside the scope of VAT e.g. non-EU supplies.

## Calculating your profit

Make sure you understand the issues touched on above before being able to count your profit. Until you have some experience and a few projects under your belt it is all too easy to miss out details that could prove very expensive in the long run.

**Use a checklist**  A good idea is to create a checklist to take with you to each viewing. List external renovations, such as roof repairs, painting, rendering, garden, entrances and leave space to make a note of the problem, solution and cost. Jot down relevant items as you go round the property. Do the same for internal renovations room by room. When you get it home it will be an invaluable aid to remind you about each property; you can add details about the alterations that need to be done and work out costings, getting quotes for each job.

The completed charts will help you calculate your renovation budget. Add this sum to the administrative and purchase costs of the property and subtract this figure from the potential sale price.

**Review calculations**  What the development is costing and, therefore, the potential profit need to be reviewed constantly because things change and you need to be aware of where to make cost cuts as the work goes forward. The initial calculation of your potential profit should be whatever is left after you have taken the purchase price, administrative costs and renovation budget off the potential sale price. The all-important calculation to make here is the total cost of the whole development.

This is a very basic calculation, but it is essential that you remember to include all costs. Don't forget you will be paying more in terms of borrowing if you run over time.

The following is an example of how costs are broken down to calculate profit.

| Purchase price | **£80,000** |
|---|---|
| Cost of works including contingency | **£25,000** |
| Purchase/sale, legal and borrowing fees | **£15,000** |
| Total costs | **£120,000** |
| Selling price | **£135,000** |
| Profit | **£15,000** |

 CHECK**LIST** MONEY

1   *Always be realistic about what you can take on financially.*

2   *Make sure you can definitely access the money for the purchase and other expenses. Research more than one possible lending scheme.*

3   *Get as much sound financial advice as possible from more than one lender or independent mortgage broker or financial advisor.*

4   *Make sure you work out a realistic budget. Calculate on the pessimistic side to avoid nasty shocks.*

5   *Keep detailed records for your accountant to calculate tax owed.*

6   *Review your calculations as to your spending regularly as the work progresses.*

# 2 the housing market

Whether you are just looking for a new home to live in and develop, buying to sell, or buying to let, getting to grips with the housing market is your first important task. Get to know which areas are on the up, the different periods of architecture and building techniques, so that you can plan a development that's in keeping with the local building style and attractive to your market. Research areas thoroughly so you can really target the sort of people who will want to live there, and, most importantly, keep your target market well in mind.

# Researching an area

The age-old adage location, location, location is as valid now as it has ever been. But along with location you need to consider the situation of any development. Where you buy your property will have an important bearing on who you will sell it to.

Properties vary enormously in style, cost and potential in different parts of the country. In some areas, particularly those where there is widespread unemployment, property may be easy and cheap to buy but difficult to sell. In other, more affluent areas, houses are much more difficult and expensive to buy. It is partly this lack of supply that forces owner-occupiers to buy unmodernised homes for premium prices, leaving no space for any profit to be made by the company or individual for doing the work.

## A site near you

When you are deciding on an area, it is best to choose somewhere near to where you live, especially if you are relatively inexperienced. You can then properly get to know the area and will be able to get a feel for the market.

## Do the research

As in any business, it is important that you get every aspect right from the beginning, so do the research. Find out what sort of properties have recently sold and for what price in the area you've chosen. You need to know all about an area in order to make a wise investment of your money and be confident you can succeed there.

## Things to beware of

Whilst you can make a profit developing any property if you buy it at the right price, there are a number of things that may affect the desirability of a property when you come to sell it. You will have to be realistic about the price and be prepared to not necessarily achieve a premium.

Factors to watch for include:
- Areas with poorly rated, problem schools.
- Proximity to electricity pylons and mobile telephone masts.
- Signs of poor council services such as abandoned cars, graffiti and litter in the streets.
- Homes near industrial areas, main roads, railway tracks, low flight paths and areas that suffer from congestion.

## Sources of information

Research is the key to successful developing and that's as true when sounding out a suitable area to buy in as when planning the actual work to the property. Sound out as many people and organisations as possible, using your phone, computer and local libraries. Always make notes.

 **KEYPOINTS** UNDERSTAND THE MARKET

*Local knowledge gives valuable insights into the sort of people who live in the area and, therefore, what sort of properties it is most logical to buy. Ask yourself the following questions:*

### Transport
- *How good is the local bus system? Do buses have low platforms to take buggies and wheelchairs?*
- *Is there a train service; how frequent and reliable is it? Do the trains run to the nearest cities?*
- *Is there an underground transport system and are there any suitable properties near to an underground station?*
- *How convenient/expensive are parking facilities?*

### Education
- *Are there plenty of good nursery schools and other pre-school facilities?*
- *Are there plenty of primary and secondary schools and what is their reputation?*
- *Are there further education colleges or language schools locally? Is there a university?*

### Amenities
- *Are there good leisure facilities such as an arts centre, museums, art galleries and libraries?*
- *Are there good sports facilities such as fitness centres, football pitches and tennis courts?*
- *Are there open green spaces such as public parks and gardens? These are highly desirable, but there could be plans to develop them into something less attractive like a shopping centre. Check with the local council to see whether they are protected areas.*
- *Are there shopping facilities/supermarkets?*
- *Are there restaurants? Are they take-aways and burger bars or upmarket, expensive restaurants?*

### Health
- *Is the area well supplied with doctors and dentists?*
- *Is there a convenient general hospital?*

## Visit the area

Once you have gained some knowledge about the property market in an area, make a trip there to see it for yourself. Spending time in your chosen location is the best way to discover all the information you need. When you are there, be proactive – make a checklist of the area's positive and negative features.

**Focus on your market**  Having considered the market in general terms, begin to focus on the actual people who are most likely to be looking for somewhere to live in the area. It is often helpful to home in on a particular group. As always, try to put yourself in their shoes. There's no point in developing an apartment up five flights of stairs with no garden for an elderly couple with a love of gardening.

 KEY**POINTS** CATEGORIES TO CONSIDER

*Students* will want good value but large enough and arranged conveniently for sharing. Gardens are not essential – good transport links and a supermarket are.

*First-time buyers* will want something at the cheaper end of the market, possibly with a small garden, transport links, shops and a supermarket.

*Business professionals* are likely to be able to afford to spend more and so will demand more. They will be looking for three- to four-bedroom homes with at least one ensuite, well-planned interiors, parking, a garden, leisure facilities, restaurants and shops.

*Most families* will require three to four bedrooms, two bathrooms, storage space, a garden and parking.

*Retired people* will probably want a smaller home on the ground floor, or a bungalow, with two or three bedrooms. An easy walk to the shops, amenities and good public transport are all desirable aspects.

# Up-and-coming areas

Every property developer strives to buy in an area fast going upmarket, and to sell a few months later at a profit. Unfortunately, this seldom happens in real life. Areas thought to be up-and-coming have a way of taking much longer to mature than predicted. So do your research and look for the signs of new affluence in the area.

**Play it safe** Look out for businesses, groups and organisations that have already done the research and have already invested. But remember that extensive commercial or large-scale housing developments can also affect the atmosphere of an area and are not necessarily seen as desirable by home-hunters.

*Make a habit of looking in estate agents' windows to get an idea of what is selling and has recently been sold and for how much.*

**Initial research** It is really worth taking time to do this initial research. Keep a notebook with you when visiting the area and note down relevant facts that might come in handy. Contact local newspapers and the property press for information on crime, local services (such as refuse collection) and parking. This will help you spot up-and-coming areas as well as good deals yourself rather than relying on estate agents to tell you.

Use professional indexes and surveys to chart trends in the marketplace. Visit your local council's planning office to view planning histories – all planning applications must be lodged there before they are approved or refused. Local groups such as Neighbourhood Watch may be able to tell you about any local issues that your estate agent has not mentioned. The vendor is legally obliged to disclose to your solicitor whether there have been any official complaints lodged about noise from any neighbourhood disputes.

There are a number of possible indicators that an area may be up-and-coming in a town or region with a quantity of unmodernised housing. These areas may be popular with mid-income home-hunters, especially if they are close to an already established area in which they aspire to live.

Handy indicators of up-and-coming areas are:
- Supermarkets, chainstores and off-licences springing up.
- Estate agents, especially those with a chain of offices, moving in to new premises – this is a sign of a healthy or recently increased turnover of domestic property.
- Major banks and building societies located on the high street.
- An increasing number of specialist businesses moving into the area, including delis, cafés and art galleries.
- The presence of new large-scale developments such as apartments and lofts.
- Major companies locating head offices, production plants or new divisions to an area. The increased employment will mean a greater demand for housing.
- Planned improvements in transport links.
- Evidence of local council or government regeneration, plans for large-scale buildings or other such initiatives.
- Properties that are in excellent condition with well-presented façades, and well-maintained gardens and outdoor spaces.
- The look of the locals – residents comprising young businesspeople and families.
- 'Fashion' –  renaming of an area by estate agents (for example, 'Brackenbury Village' instead of just 'Hammersmith'), may make some people think more highly of an area.

# Building techniques

Learning to recognise different building techniques and materials can save a lot of time and hassle when planing any conversion. Building methods have changed progressively over the years. Unti the 1930s most walls were built in solid brickwork. Cavity walls were introduced in about 1930 but were not used for all pre-war housing. Foundation details were not specified in by-laws until about 1914, although many houses prior to that did have brick footings.

## Older traditional

This describes housing stock built from the late-19th century until the end of World War II. It includes small, terraced houses and Arts and Crafts and Edwardian houses from the 19th century to larger semi-detached homes, terraced houses with two to five floors and a basement or cellar, and blocks of flats from four-to eight-storeys high. All these would be built of regionally produced bricks. Many were rendered to cover unsightly brickwork. Roofs are usually of slates or tiles. There may be no damp-proof courses.

## Modern traditional

This describes properties built since World War II and includes terraced and semi-detached houses as well as blocks of flats. Tiles and bricks are not necessarily made from local materials. Some blocks of flats have flat timber or concrete roofs covered with asphalt or layers of roofing felt. Houses are usually two-storeys high and flats up to six storeys. Post-war properties generally have cavity walls on concrete foundations with a damp-proof course.

## Rationalised traditional

This covers a range of construction methods which used traditional materials and building techniques, but in a way that improved the efficiency of the construction process. It includes cross-wall construction, which describes masonry load-bearing gable and separating walls with infill panels for front and rear elevations.

### Industrialised building

A range of systems was developed in the 1960s for low-, medium- and high-rise housing. These were built mainly by local authorities. There were many different structural styles including timber-framed panels, steel frames with infill panels and precast concrete panels.

# Listed buildings

The listing scheme was created in 1950 to give protection to buildings of special architectural or historic interest in England and Wales. Listing covers all features within the boundaries of the property. Historic association with people and events of national importance, construction methods and rarity value are also criteria. There are three grades for listing: Grade I; Grade II* and Grade II.

Buildings of high quality and character, or designed by nationally recognised architects from 1840–1914, are listed, as are high-quality buildings from the period 1914–1939. Outstanding buildings built post-1939 may also be listed but they have to be at least 30 years old. The same situation now exists in Wales, Scotland and Northern Ireland.

### Your responsibility

If the building is listed, whatever its Grade, you will need to get listed building consent from your local council if you want to demolish it or any part of it, or make any alterations that would affect its character inside or out. Repairs that match exactly may not need consent, but your local council will advise you on this as other minor repairs may need consent. Contact your local planning department as soon as possible to discuss whether an application is required. Listing does not automatically stop you from making changes. It ensures that what you propose will be given consideration. Obtaining consent takes time, so don't leave it until the last minute.

Work that will need consent includes: changing windows and doors; painting over brickwork or removing external surfaces; putting in dormer windows or roof lights; putting up aerials, satellite dishes and burglar alarms; changing roofing materials; moving or removing internal walls; making new doorways; and removing or altering fireplaces, panelling or staircases.

Carrying out unauthorised work to a listed building is a criminal offence. In addition the local council can require you to put the building back as it was. Ultimately, if you do not have the money to reinstate/repair the listed building English Heritage/ the local council have the right to carry out essential repair works on your behalf and bill you for it.

---

## ✓ CHECK**LIST** THE HOUSING MARKET

1   *Decide on an area, preferably a site near you.*

2   *Research the area, including getting information on transport, education, amenities, health facilities, and spotting an up-and-coming area.*

3   *Use as many local information sources as possible, including estate agents, newspapers and property publications, the council, local groups and the Internet.*

4   *Target your market: students and first-time buyers, business professionals, families and retired people will all want different things.*

5   *Run your business efficiently. Do your sums, get professional advice and be realistic.*

6   *Recognise types of building and house styles. Understand what's involved if you buy a listed building or a building in a Conservation Area.*

# 3 buying a property

When buying a property there are many considerations, including whether you should buy freehold or leasehold, where you should buy, the problems of finding a solicitor, getting a structural survey and making use of such a survey. Don't set your heart on one particular property until you have completed the purchase. Many things can go wrong, especially if there is a chain of purchasers, so don't commit to any advance expense that relies on your purchase going ahead. Be patient – the whole process may take longer than you expect.

# Freehold or leasehold

It is important that you know the difference between a freehold property and a leasehold one.

## Buying freehold

Most houses are freehold. This means that you legally own and are responsible for the house and its grounds. As such, it is your job to maintain the property and check the professional status of any workmen you employ. You will need to be aware of any by-laws that may govern what you do, for example, whether the property is in a Conservation Area, or whether the building you want to buy is listed. In multiple occupancy properties residents may join together and purchase the freehold to ensure the property is cared for as they would wish.

# Buying leasehold

The majority of flats are sold on a leasehold basis. This means you have bought a lease, which allows you to live in the property for a certain length of time. The actual owner of the building is the person or company who owns the freehold and you will have to pay them an annual ground rent. They are then responsible for the maintenance and upkeep of the building. For this service they will expect you to pay additional service charges for which they should arrange buildings insurance, cleaning and general maintenance. The cost of extra works, such as the redecoration of communal areas or roof repairs or new lifts will usually be split between the number of leaseholders in the building. Be sure to find out the details of the lease at the viewing stage.

 KEY**POINTS** FINDING A PROPERTY

*At first glance there may be plenty of potential properties, but on closer inspection you may find that few of these will be cost effective by the time you've done them up and sold them on. The initial stages of sourcing a property are:*

1 *Researching an area.*

2 *Finding a property.*

3 *Viewing a property.*

4 *Arranging a survey.*

*The first thing is to choose the area you want to buy in. You may try to find an up-and-coming area but it is difficult to make sure you're hitting it at exactly the right time (see pages 35–6). If possible choose an area near to where you live so you can spend time there and really get to know it.*

# Ways of finding a property

Estate agents are the obvious first port of call when looking for a property. Register with all agents in the area who will send details via e-mail and post. You will soon get to recognise the jargon and what to expect from estate agents' descriptions and pick out just those that seem relevant to your project.

## Driving around the area

A useful way when you are just starting out, and if you have time, is to drive around a particular area and look at properties with 'for sale' signs. You can dismiss immediately those in impossible locations and home in on those that look promising. This may be time-consuming and costly but it can be very educational. For example, if there seem to be many homes for sale in one area, there may be some reason that people are not buying there.

## Local press

Scour the local papers and property magazines for properties, some of which may be for private sale.

## Buying at auction

This is a way of buying a property at a competitive price, but be warned, buying at auction is a skill that has to be learned. If you are not careful or have not been to an auction before, you could get carried away and end up bidding over the odds for a property. You must do your research. Find out as much as possible about the property you are interested in well in advance of the auction. Visit an auction house to sit in on a few property lots before you actually go to buy so that you understand how auctions work. To find out where and when auctions in your area are held see local press or the Internet.

Always give yourself a top price and do not allow yourself to go over that, no matter how tempted you are. If the bidding gets too high, get up and leave. If nobody else is interested in the property you may be able to pick up a bargain, although this hardly ever happens. Properties sold at auction can be very risky as they are often run-down and require major structural work. If you buy on a whim, you can end up paying over the odds for a property that turns out to be a liability. Remember, once the hammer goes down you are legally obliged to buy the property and you must complete within four weeks.

## The Internet

This can be an absolutely fascinating way of looking for property. It can also be very time-consuming. Pick an area and stick to it otherwise you can too easily get seduced by properties not conveniently nearby which would be a drain on your resources and energy and fail to bring in that essential profit.

## Buying off-plan

This means buying a property that has yet to be built. The best way to find out about these is via the property press. Contact the developers to see artists' impressions of the finished scheme and find out about their previous projects. Visiting these will give you a feel for the developer's design style. Make sure you have a list of agreed internal fixtures and fittings from the developer in writing.

*Buying off-plan will give you the opportunity to choose the layout and view you like best – and you can often get a good deal*.

The developer usually asks for a reservation fee when you choose your home so they can show their financier they have a certain number of sales. This frees up their cash flow and allows them to offer the property at a cheaper price than when the scheme is completed. If the market is good your investment may have increased before you move in.

You may also benefit from discounted deals your developer can take advantage of for fittings and furnishings. These are often fashionable and can also add value to the property. If the area is on the way up, you could be investing where prices are about to rise. However, if the market drops, you are obliged to complete at the same purchase price.

## Buying privately

Small ads in local papers and on the Internet offer private property sales. This could possibly save you a few thousand pounds if the vendors are looking for a quick sale and they deduct their saving in agents' fees from the asking price. Don't assume, however, that a private sale is automatically a bargain. The disadvantages are that it is you who will be working for any financial saving. If you decide to pursue a private sale be sure you are clear about what you expect to be included in the sale and confirm any verbal agreements in writing.

*You may waste time viewing properties that are unrealistically described and will need to deal with the vendor directly.*

## Buy ex-council stock

Look for brick-built properties with roofs and windows in good condition and lots of private homes nearby.

## Buy outside the peak periods

Most people buy properties in spring and autumn so you may find a bargain in winter or summer when the few people selling may want a quick sale.

## Consider repossessions

These properties may well be in a poor state of repair but the mortgage lender will be keen to sell quickly and so a cheaper price may be negotiable (although the law says that lenders must get the 'best price reasonably obtainable').

*Take your time* to consider a number of properties and learn to recognise what you are looking at and what you are looking for:

- Don't jump at the first property you see because it has a pretty front door.
- Dress comfortably; wear trainers or walking shoes.
- Make notes and take a camcorder or camera to record your viewings; but always ask permission from the vendors first.
- Don't be rushed, think it through thoroughly.

*View as many* likely properties as you can. It's the best way of getting a feeling for when a property is sound and when it isn't, whether it's being offered at a good price compared to other property, and you can make sure that you like the location. Be wary of:

- Properties on busy roads.
- Flats in basements.
- Properties that need too much costly renovation. This might seem to indicate value for money, but often disadvantages outweigh advantages.

*Inspect the exterior* of the property carefully. Get to recognise potentially expensive external works that will be needed, such as rotten window frames, bad pointing, loose gutters and cracked or missing roof tiles. Stand well back from the house and check:

- Whether it is horizontally and vertically aligned, whether the windows are level and whether there are any major cracks in the brickwork. (These all indicate that there may be subsidence or structural instability.)
- That chimneys are standing up straight.
- That there is a damp-proof course.

*Check that the interior* of the property has been well cared for. Badly done DIY jobs, poorly finished paintwork and attempts to mask problems are all warning signs. Look out for the following:

- Get to recognise the smell of damp and rot and watch out for damp patches on walls or ceilings.
- Do the floorboards feel spongy?
- Can you see any fungus lurking in dark corners?
- Is there any unsatisfactory plumbing? Ask about the age and condition of the boiler.
- Look for expensive items that need updating such as new window frames (are the windows double-glazed?), new flooring or a new bathroom suite.
- Are there enough power points? Find out when the house was last rewired.

**Ask lots of questions** when you are viewing properties, for example:

- What will be included in the sale, for instance, the shed in the garden, the light fittings, any shelves, fitted carpets? If they are included and you don't want them, find out if you could get a reduction.
- Are the walls and roof insulated?
- How much does it cost to heat the house in winter?
- Is there a selling chain? If the vendors are waiting to move into another house before they sell, you could wait a very long time before completing.

**Make a second visit** if a property meets most of your criteria on the first viewing. Take a very good look at the basic structure and condition of the property. Take a friend or parent with you. A second opinion can be invaluable and may prevent you from making an expensive mistake. It's even better if he or she has experience in buying or renovating property.

**Be aware of development sites** surrounding your property and check the planning records. Planning control seeks to protect residential amenity, for example, the amount of light into habitable rooms, but there is no right to a view in planning law. So if the unrestricted view of the river is what you bought a house for, make sure that permission has not been granted for any development in the way.

# The buying process

Buying a house is a complicated business and the process usually takes a few months. It usually happens more or less in the following order:

- Making an offer
- Getting a valuation.
- Getting a survey or homebuyer's report.
- Doing the legal preparation (conveyancing).
- Exchanging contracts and paying a deposit.
- Completing the sale.

## Making an offer

This is a process of negotiation and it is rare for the asking price to be the final price. Estate agents deliberately mark the property artificially high since it is taken for granted that negotiation will take place. The first offer is usually 5–10% below the asking price, depending on the perceived level of demand and market conditions. The two sides then work towards a price somewhere in the middle.

**Market value**  Before making an offer be sure that you know the market value of the property. It's worth finding out what properties have actually sold for in the area, rather than the price that they were valued at. You are not restricted to making an offer on only one property but if all your offers are accepted you will have to make a decision very quickly.

**Subject to contract**  If your offer is accepted it will then be 'subject to contract'. This means you and the seller have agreed in principle to go ahead with the transaction but neither of you is legally bound.

**Terms of the offer**  Make sure the vendor and agent are both aware of the terms of your offer. For example, which fixtures and fittings you want to be included and what work you want to be done before the sale is completed. Make sure the offer is subject to a survey and contract. If the survey shows something that needs doing on the property, renegotiate. If a large amount of work needs to be done on the property this may have been factored into the price, but sometimes it is not.

**Reduce the risk of gazumping**  Ask the vendor to take the house off the market immediately to discourage any further offers.

# Valuations and surveys

Once you have found a property, secured your mortgage and briefed your solicitor, it is time to think about an independent surveyor's report. It is tempting to dismiss the need for this with so many other costs, but currently it is your responsibility as buyer to find out what you are committing yourself to (although new legislation has been proposed). The seller has no liability once the purchase is completed.

Surveys are designed to give you the information you need to make an informed and sensible property purchase. The Consumer's Association and the Council of Mortgage Lenders both advise you to arrange a survey before buying a property. There are three main types of survey:

- Basic valuation.
- Homebuyer's survey and valuation report (HSV).
- Full structural survey (also called Building survey.

When money is tight, the idea of spending more than the bare minimum may not be desirable, but a survey is essential if you are buying an old property or one that needs any degree of renovation. Do not rely on just a valuation.

## A valuation

A valuation, or 'basic valuation' as it is often called, is an inspection carried out on behalf of your mortgage lender. Its purpose is to check that your intended property is worth at least the amount they are lending you and to identify any problems that could affect the security of the loan. You will be expected to pay for this valuation. In addition to the cost of the valuation itself, you may also be charged an administration or arrangement fee by your bank or building society. You are entitled to know the amount of the fee being paid to the surveyor and the amount being retained by the lender.

A valuation is not a survey, it is a limited inspection. A property can have defects that are not of concern to the mortgage lender and, therefore, won't appear in a valuation report. Furthermore, a valuation does not provide you with any legal recourse as it is for the benefit of the lender only.

*A survey does give you a certain amount of legal recourse and, most importantly, it is conducted for the benefit of the borrower rather than the lender.*

**Surveyors responsibilities** Surveyors should comment on all parts of a property that are readily accessible but they are not obliged to inspect areas that are difficult to get at. They won't lift carpets, shift furniture, use a ladder to inspect the roof or move items stored in the loft unless you instruct them to do so. Similarly, since most surveyors are not trained electricians or plumbers, they will not test services such as the wiring and water supply. However, they may comment on their condition. Where necessary, surveyors will recommend that an expert examination be carried out.

**Survey results** Read the terms and conditions of the survey carefully and double-check with your surveyor if you are unclear about anything. Use the results to make an informed judgement as to whether to proceed with the purchase and to assess whether the property is a reasonable purchase at the agreed price. Be clear what decisions and courses of action should be taken before contracts are exchanged.

# Homebuyer's report

The Homebuyer's Survey and Valuation Report (HSV) is a service carried out to a standard format defined by the Royal Institution of Chartered Surveyors (RICS). The HSV is primarily designed for properties built within the last 150 years, which are of conventional construction and in reasonable condition. An HSV does give you legal recourse but is not a detailed survey of every aspect of the property. It focuses only on significant and urgent matters.

 KEY**POINTS** HSV REPORT

*An HSV seeks information on the following:*

1   *The property's general condition.*

2   *Urgent and significant matters that need assessing before entering into exchanging contracts (or before making an offer in Scotland) including recommendations for any further specialist inspectors.*

3   *Any significant defects in accessible parts of the property, which may affect its value.*

4   *Results of any testing of walls for dampness.*

5   *General comments on damage to timbers, including woodworm or rot and evidence of damp.*

6   *Comments on the existence and condition of damp-proofing, insulation and drainage (although the latter will not be tested).*

7   *The recommended reinstatement cost for insurance purposes. This means the anticipated costs of reconstructing a building in the event of its damage by an insured risk such as fire. It is not the same as the market value of the property.*

8   *The value of the property on the open market.*

## Full structural survey

Also known as a building survey, this is an in-depth and comprehensive inspection suitable for all properties but especially recommended for the following buildings:

- All listed buildings.
- Properties built before 1900.
- Any building constructed in an unusual way, regardless of age.
- A property you are planning to dramatically renovate or alter.
- Properties that have already had extensive alterations and work done.

A building survey generally includes the following:

- All major and minor faults.
- Implications of any defects and cost of repairs.
- Results of testing walls for dampness and testing timbers for damage including woodworm or rot.
- Comments on damp-proofing, insulation and drainage (although the latter will not be tested).
- Extensive technical information on the construction of the property and materials used.
- Information on the location.
- Recommendations for any specialist inspections.

## How to find a surveyor

You may find that your mortgage lender or estate agent can recommend a surveyor. It is worth asking whether they have a working relationship with one. In choosing your surveyor, it is important that you select someone who is a member of the Royal Institution of Chartered Surveyors. They can be identified by the letters MRICS or FRICS (or TechRICS for technical surveyors) after their name. Chartered surveyors have undertaken an extensive period of training and are all required to carry professional indemnity insurance.

Because a full survey is a bespoke service, you should discuss your exact requirements with your surveyor before he or she visits the property. You may find it helpful to meet him or her at the property, after the survey is complete, to discuss the findings.

# Conveyancing

Conveyancing is the legal business of buying and selling a property. For this you will need a legal adviser, usually a solicitor, but it is possible to use someone who is registered with the Council for Licensed Conveyancers instead. Many lenders or estate agents can provide a list of solicitors for you to choose from. You can get details of other solicitors from the Law Society or the Council for Licensed Conveyancers. Solicitors' fees vary so it's worth getting a few estimates. Check that fees include VAT and expenses.

**Choosing a solicitor**  Don't necessarily go for a solicitor who happens to be nearby or is recommended by your estate agent. Ask friends or relatives whether they have recently used a solicitor for conveyancing with whom they were happy. The most important thing is that they are reliable and efficient as they will be representing your interests. Remember to ask the solicitor for a breakdown of their conveyancing fees before you give them the go-ahead to do any work on your behalf.

## Solicitor's responsibilities

A solicitor will act on the client's behalf in all matters. The first thing your solicitor will do is get a copy of the Land Registry entry (or the title deeds if the property isn't registered) from the seller's solicitor. These are the legal documents giving evidence of ownership. They are written in legal jargon and need to be carefully examined to make sure there are no unreasonable conditions about how you use the property. If you are buying a leasehold property (which includes most flats) your solicitor will also need to check the lease to find out who has to arrange (and pay for) insuring the building, how much ground rent you will have to pay after the sale, how service charges (for repairs and maintenance) are calculated and whether service charges and ground rent can be increased and if so, how. If there is a problem with the lease it should be sorted out before contracts are exchanged. If you have lost out financially because of your solicitor or conveyancer, you can complain to the Office for the Supervision of Solicitors or the Council for Licensed Conveyancers. You may be able to get compensation.

## Land Registry checks

Your solicitor will check with the Land Registry that the seller has the right to sell the property and, when the sale goes ahead, will register your ownership and mortgage agreement with the Registry. You have to pay fees for this, which vary depending on the property price and if it is already registered or not. He/she will also carry out local council and other searches, including:

- Checking that no alterations have been made without planning permission.
- Establishing whether the street, pavement and drains are public and council maintained.
- Finding out whether there are any other expenses linked to the property such as a right-to-buy discount that must be repaid.
- Checking that there are no disputes about things such as noise or parking with neighbours.
- Making sure that the property's boundaries are clear and that there is no disagreement about maintaining them.
- Checking that a motorway is not about to be built in the adjacent field or that there are any other plans that might affect the value of the property.

The contract is drawn up by the seller's solicitor and involves supplying pre-contract information such as any fixtures and fittings that are to be included in the sale price and answering a standard set of enquires on the property being sold. The solicitor will organise exchange of contracts, the transfer of monies (including a deposit), calling down the buyer's mortgage loan and paying off the seller's mortgage, and will organise the transfer of title deeds, ultimately to the buyer or their lender.

# Stamp duty

Stamp duty is a government tax that you may
have to pay if the property you are buying costs
over £60,000. Some areas of the country are exempt
from stamp duty. You should pay stamp duty only on
the price of the property itself, not on fixtures and
fittings such as curtains or appliances, so it is best
to pay for these things separately.

## FACTS&FIGURES STAMP DUTY

*The most significant duties are based on the
amount of consideration. For land transactions
and lease premiums rates are charged on the
whole consideration.*

| | |
|---|---|
| *Up to £60,000* | **nil** |
| *£60,001 to £250,000* | **1%** |
| *£150,001 to £500,000* | **3%** |
| *More than £500,000* | **4%** |

# Preparing and exchanging contracts

When all the details have been checked, the
contract will be negotiated. This stage can often
involve long delays as the seller may not agree to
everything. For example, you may want to pay less
than the price you originally offered, or get the seller
to carry out repairs. All the conditions of the sale
need to be agreed before contracts are exchanged.
Solicitors negotiate on your behalf but will need to
be in regular contact to discuss any changes.

**Signing the contract** When the contract is drawn
up and agreed, you can sign it. The seller signs an
identical contract and your respective conveyancers

swap the signed documents in what's known as 'exchange of contracts'. At this point both you and the seller become legally bound. You will have to pay a deposit at this stage, usually 10% of the purchase price, but it can be less if the seller agrees. You could lose the deposit if you pull out after exchanging contracts.

## Gazumping

During negotiations, the seller could accept a better offer from another buyer before you have exchanged contracts. To avoid gazumping you may be able to persuade the seller, through your solicitor, to sign an agreement that the sale can't be called off if contracts are exchanged within a certain time. There may be extra legal fees for this.

---

*£* **FACTS&FIGURES** HOW LONG TO BUY?

*According to research carried out in 2003 in England and Wales, the average time taken from starting house-hunting to completing a purchase is 22 weeks.*

| | |
|---|---|
| *From beginning your property hunt to your offer being accepted* | **12 weeks** |
| *From acceptance of offer to offer of mortgage* | **4 weeks** |
| *From mortgage offer to exchange of contracts* | **4 weeks** |
| *From exchange of contracts to completion* | **2–4 weeks** |

# Buying in Scotland

In Scotland most properties are sold through solicitors rather than estate agents, a though the number of estate agencies has increased in recent years. Solicitors are able to call themselves 'Solicitors and Estate Agents' and some set up 'Solicitors' Property Centres', where cetails of all properties being sold by solicitors in the area can be found. The centres are financed by subscriptions from the member solicitors and by charges made to sellers of property – as in the UK, the service is free to prospective buyers. Other solicitors' firms have their own property department and employ sales staff to deal with the non-legal aspects of buying and selling in these offices.

All types of property are widely advertised in the Scottish press and on the Internet.

*A list of buildings for sale in Scotland with historical or architectural importance is issued quarterly by The Historic Buildings Bureau.*

In Scotland, if you are interested in buying a property that you have seen at a property centre or a solicitor's, you will be directed to the solicitor actually selling it. You will also need a solicitor for conveyancing. English solicitors are not able to practise in Scotland, so if you are relocating from outside Scotland, ask your usual solicitor whether they have a Scottish contact or recommendation.

**The Law Society of Scotland** This organisation also produces a 'Directory of General Services', listing the contact details of practising solicitors throughout Scotland, as well as brochures detailing all of the relevant procedures and legalities. Be warned, there is no scale of solicitors' fees in Scotland – shop around for a competitive estimate.

## How properties are priced

Generally, properties are presented for sale at 'offers over' a stated figure. Depending on demand for a property, the price eventually paid may be considerably higher than the original figure; it is rare for a purchaser to pay the asking price or below. Sometimes properties are offered at a fixed price, usually because the owner wants a quick sale or the property hasn't sold at an 'offers over' price. In this instance a buyer should be ready to proceed very quickly, as the first acceptable offer at the stated price will secure the property.

## The buying procedure

When you tell your solicitor that you are interested in buying a particular property he or she will 'note interest', that is, tell the seller's solicitor that you are interested in the property. You should then have a chance to make an offer, although the seller is not legally obliged to give you that chance. Ask your solicitor if the mortgage lender is happy to use the same solicitor as you for their legal work. This keeps costs down. Get an itemised estimate of what he or she will charge before you go ahead.

*Ask your solicitor if the mortgage lender is happy to use the same solicitor as you for their legal work. This will help to keep costs down.*

The process of obtaining a mortgage in Scotland is similar to that in England and most of the major English banks and building societies and all the Scottish banks will lend on the security of Scottish properties. As the buying process can move very quickly it's wise to make sure the necessary finance will be available when you need it – subject always to a satisfactory survey on the chosen property.

However, in Scotland it is usual to have a survey carried out before you make an offer for a property.

If your offer is accepted you are bound to proceed with the purchase and it will be too late to discover defects or that you cannot get a loan on the property. This does mean that if your offer is unsuccessful you will have wasted the survey fee. Your solicitor will usually suggest that the survey takes place once you have told him or her you are interested in buying the property.

## Making an offer

When your mortgage company is happy with the valuation of the property, they will issue you an 'offer of advance'. If you are also happy with the surveyor's report, the next thing to do is to make an offer – usually through your solicitor. On a fixed-price property the seller will take the first offer received for the fixed amount. However, most sellers ask for 'offers over' a certain amount and set a 'closing date' by which offers have to be made. Your solicitor will prepare a letter setting out your offer and will send it to the seller's solicitor.

When making an offer you must specify all the conditions under which you want to buy the property and also how much you wish to pay. Prices quoted as 'offers over' usually mean another 10–15% on the price quoted. Your solicitor will guide you on how much you should offer – this is where a solicitor with knowledge of the local market can be particularly useful. In your offer you must also state when you want to move into the property, although this can be further negotiated with the seller at a later date.

## Acceptance of offer

Once your offer has been accepted, the property is yours. This is one advantage of the system of house purchase in Scotland, in that it more or less prevents gazumping. When the details of the offer are sorted out between the two parties' solicitors, letters are exchanged between them, which create a legally binding contract. These are known in Scotland as the 'missives' and are the equivalent to the exchange of contracts in England and Wales. So, whether your offer is successful or not, you know where you stand very quickly. This is another advantage of the Scottish property-buying system.

*Once your offer is accepted, the property is yours. This is one advantage of the system of house purchase in Scotland, in that it more or less prevents gazumping.*

When your solicitor has concluded the missives, the conveyancing process will be finalised and you will complete any outstanding loan application papers. Your solicitor will then meet the seller's solicitor and hand over a cheque for the full price in exchange for the title deeds, which he will then hand over to you.

If you buy in Scotland and intend to make the property your principal residence you will acquire Scottish domicile. It is advisable to consult a solicitor at this point, as it may affect, among other things, the way the property is inherited when you die.

# Buying in Ireland (Eire)

In Ireland it is common to buy a property in a number of different ways: through an estate agent, privately or at an auction. Your solicitor will obtain draft contracts and a copy of the title deeds from the seller's solicitors. You must then sign and return the contract to the seller's solicitor, along with a deposit (which is normally 10% of the purchase price) so that the contracts can be counter-signed by the seller. As soon as these contracts have been signed by both parties and the deposit paid there is a binding agreement requiring the seller to hand over possession and you to hand over the balance on the closing date stated in the contract.

Once a binding agreement is in existence a list of closing documents is set out, all of which must be handed over by the seller's solicitor in exchange for the balance. Prior to closing the transaction your solicitor should make relevant enquiries to establish, for instance, that there are no judgements that are still affecting the property, or orders against the seller or any adverse registrations pending against the property.

Your solicitor will normally visit the offices of the seller's solicitor with a bank draft for the balance. This will be handed over only when the closing documents are found to be in order and the searches are found to be clear. You become the owner when the bank draft is exchanged for all these documents. Keys are then handed over and you can take possession of your new home.

---

 CHECK**LIST** BUYING

**Leasehold or freehold?** *Understand the difference and the advantages and disadvantages of each.*

**Choose an area.** *If you will be managing the development, an area close to where you live makes sense.*

**Explore estate agents,** *local press, buying at auction, the Internet and other purchasing possibilities.*

**View the property.** *Take your time; if interested view a second time; ask the right questions.*

**Understand the buying process.** *Organising your finances, making an offer, finding a surveyor, getting valuations and surveys.*

**Conveyancing:** *understanding your solicitor's responsibilities; preparing and exchanging contracts.*

# 4 planning the project

It is important to make sure that the basic structure of the building is sound before you start planning to alter the interior spaces. Before purchasing the property you should have assessed the extent of work required to make it perfect for your potential market. Don't be daunted by extensive repairs. Make the property safe and sound first. If you have done your calculations correctly, you should have the resources to get the job done properly.

# A realistic budget

It cannot be stressed too much that the first thing to do is to work out a realistic budget for your development and stick to it. Itemise the work you intend to do and cost each individual item. If some things turn out to be more expensive than planned, make up for this by saving money on some other item of work. You can often get brilliant ideas from expensive showrooms or magazines and then the skill is to get a similar effect with less costly materials.

**Home improvement grants** It may be worth finding out if you are eligible for a home improvement grant from your local authority for some aspect of the work you are considering; grants are generally only available to home-owners, not developers. Each authority will have its own rules about types of help it will offer and about the conditions you must meet in order to qualify for help.

# The structure

Before purchasing your property you should have assessed the extent of the repairs, work and decoration required to make it perfect for your market. And before you actually begin on the interior layout and design, you should make sure it is safe and sound and in a good state of repair. There is no point in spending lots of money on cosmetic repairs if you have not carried out the basic repairs. Ensuring the basic structure of the property is in good condition is one of the most important improvements you will make, and potential buyers who are paying a premium for a hassle-free home will expect just that.

The first thing is to consider any repairs that are mentioned in the building survey. These should be done before you even think about any interior planning and design work. For example, the state

## KEY**POINTS** STRUCTURAL POINTS

*Building methods and materials change over time. The dates below are guidelines as to when changes were introduced and may help to eliminate some of the more obvious questions when considering defects in older properties.*

| | |
|---|---|
| Damp-proof courses | **1900–1920 onwards** |
| Cavity walls | **1930–1940 onwards** |
| Reinforced concrete floors | **1920 onwards** |
| Concrete tiled roofs | **mostly from 1940 onwards** |
| Copper plumbing | **1945 onwards** |
| 13-amp ring mains | **1947 onwards** |

1910  1920  1930  1940  1950  1960  1970  1980

of the drains, the state of the roof, damp-proofing, window frames, cracks in walls and pointing of brickwork, and electric wiring. Where indicated by a survey, you should treat against woodworm, dry rot and damp. These things are not cheap but they are necessary and need to be budgeted for.

Once the property is a watertight, functioning shell you can consider how it can be arranged and redeveloped for resale.

## Structural points to consider

The difference between new-build and older properties is that new-build will have a consistent construction method throughout, whereas most older properties will have evolved over time. As a result, older buildings are often a mixture of original and later construction, with a combination of different materials, methods and standards.

The following are some of the differences you may find between old and new purpose-built properties or within various parts of a refurbished unit.

**Foundations** In houses built before 1914 load-bearing brick walls were often built directly off the subsoil without concrete strip footings, or off paving slabs, although sometimes the brickwork of the wall was stepped out at the base to spread the load.

In more recent houses there is always some form of widening at the base of the wall unless it is built on very hard ground or rock.

Settlement and damage to foundations can be caused by movement between old and new foundations or by subsidence. The latter can be due to heavy rain or drought on a clay subsoil, or the removal of large trees, which changes the water content of the soil in the area of their roots.

**Walls** External walls before 1930 are usually of solid brickwork 9in or 13½in thick. Houses built after 1930 usually have cavity walls or solid walls faced with tiles or boarding. Or they may be built from timber-framed panels or concrete. Many older mansion blocks use solid wall construction although some have a concrete or steel frame with panel walls or brick cladding. A brick facing does not necessarily mean the full thickness of the wall is of brick.

Damage to the mortar between the bricks from weather or penetration by moisture may mean you need to repoint or replace individual bricks.

*In the restoration of an old house, badly eroded brickwork may have to be rendered or treated to resist damp penetration.*

Internal walls in old and new houses may be constructed from timber-stud, brick, breeze or concrete block. Where new openings have been made in internal walls, the construction above may be supported on timber, steel or concrete beams. In modernised properties walls may have been lined with waterproof lathing to protect internal finishes.

**Floors**  Ground floors in old houses were often constructed of timber floorboards resting on a honeycomb sleeper of walls. The space under such floors should be well ventilated to prevent rot.

Modern houses usually have solid concrete floors. If ground-level timber floors are replaced by solid concrete floors, it is essential that sufficient air flow is maintained to adjoining timber floors.

**Roofs**  As Britain has high rainfall, the most logical roof construction is a pitched tiled roof. If properly constructed, and barring storm damage, this form of roof should last around 80 years. Older pitched roofs may be tiled or slated and were often built without sarking felt or boards. They may have suffered from neglect where gutters haven't been cleared and lead flashings haven't been maintained; incorrectly repaired roofs may allow water to reach the rafters, causing decay. The problems could remain if the roof is only repaired rather than totally replaced.

# Building Regulations

The Building Regulations are a set of minimum requirements designed to ensure that any work you do on the property is safe and legal. Although it may not be necessary to get planning permission to carry out work, any work must always adhere to current Building Regulations. It is a criminal offence to carry out any work on a property that fails to comply. Not only that, but you are legally required to declare any work you have carried out on the property when you come to sell it. If you do not have the correct Building Regulation approval, potential buyers may be advised to insist on a price reduction or, worse still, to withdraw from the sale.

Consult the Building Regulations department at your local council planning office before embarking on any building work. Ask for a copy of their guidelines and relevant application forms.

## KEY**POINTS** BUILDING REGULATIONS

*The types of work for which you must have Building Regulations approval include:*

- *Any extension, loft or cellar conversions.*
- *Anything that affects the structure of the building such as the removal of a load-bearing wall.*
- *Bathrooms or kitchens in new locations.*
- *Installation of heating appliances (not electric).*
- *New chimneys or flues.*
- *Underpinning or work that affects foundations.*
- *Altered openings for new windows in roofs/walls.*
- *Replacing roof coverings (unless like-for-like).*
- *Installation of cavity insulation.*
- *Erection of buildings in the property's grounds.*

Submit the relevant paperwork: either a building notice or full application with detailed plans, elevations and sections showing the proposed work, together with a site plan. A Building Regulations Officer will visit your site to make sure it is running in accordance with the guidelines, and a Building Regulations Approval Certificate will be issued on the satisfactory completion of works.

# Planning permission

For many home improvements planning permission is not required, while for others, even quite minor things such as replacing windows, you do need to gain approval before you can begin. Whatever type of house you live in, the rule is always check with the local planning department before embarking on any work. If you build something which needs planning permission without obtaining permission first, you may be forced to put things right later. This could be troublesome and also a very costly mistake.

You can make certain minor changes without planning permission. These are called 'permitted development rights'. In some areas these are more restricted. For example, in Conservation Areas or Areas of Outstanding Natural Beauty or National Parks you do need planning permission for certain types of work, which you don't need in other areas.

Examples of when you need planning permission:
- To divide off part of the property as a separate home, for example, to create a self-contained flat.
- To build a separate house in the garden.
- To build a parking space for a commercial vehicle or divide the property into separate work and living accommodation.
- If work might obstruct the view of the road access.
- For a new/wider access to a trunk/classified road.
- For an extension beyond development rights.

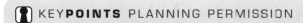

# KEY**POINTS** PLANNING PERMISSION

*If you decide not to employ an architect, here's what you need to do:*

1   *Visit the council for planning application forms.*

2   *Draw up relevant scale drawings of your existing and proposed dwelling. Generally, these drawings need to be 100% accurate so don't do them yourself unless you are totally confident!*

3   *Submit the plans and application forms to the council with the appropriate fee. Await acknowledgement of receipt of application.*

4   *The council will write to the properties in your immediate locality and/or place a notice on your property about the proposed changes. These home-owners have 21 days in which to see the plans for themselves and to lodge any objection. If the council receives more than two objections then the decision will go to a committee.*

5   *Planning permission will either be granted or refused. If refused, you could appeal, but the appeal's decision may not be any different and you could end up paying costs. Instead, you could listen to the council's comments, revise your plans and resubmit your application.*

6   *If permission is granted and, if during work being carried out you want to make any minor changes to the original and approved plans, you must submit the amendment to the council.*

7   *If the changes are thought to be insignificant, you can continue with the work; if significant, and you go ahead with the new plans, then you may recieve an enforcement notice to stop work, or they may insist on a retrospective application.*

8   *If your new planning application is not granted you must undo whatever work has been done so that it complies with your original plans.*

# Neighbours and party walls

Before you start on your development it is best to inform your neighbours about the work, even if what you are going to do is perfectly legal. If your plans will affect party walls you may need a surveyor or lawyer to advise on a Party Wall Agreement.

A party wall is a wall that separates buildings on either side of the boundary. A party structure is a floor partition between flats and maisonettes that are approached by separate staircases or entrances. So, like party walls, they form part of a building.

Works to the party walls are covered under the Party Wall Act 1996, and require certain procedures to be followed. Failure to follow these procedures can extensively delay your project and, in some cases, lead to detailed redesign being required. A chartered building surveyor will be able to give advice in this regard and act as a party wall surveyor.

## Informing your neighbours

You must serve the notice on your neighbours at least two months before you start the work on party walls or a month for party fence walls or excavations that are close to your neighbours' property. The notice is only valid for one year. Give the neighbours

 KEY**POINTS** PARTY WALL ACT

*If the Party Wall Act is relevant in your case, you must inform your neighbours of the work that is to take place. Work under the Party Wall Act includes:*

- *Works to an existing wall or structure shared with another property.*
- *Building on a boundary.*
- *Excavating near a neighbouring building.*

your name and address, the building's address if it is different from your own, a clear statement that your notice of intention to undertake the work is under the Party Wall Act, full details of the proposed works and the date you intend to start work.

*The Party Wall Act gives guidelines for resolving disputes between neighbours in relation to their party walls.*

After the notice is served, your neighbour has up to 14 days to give written consent for the work to take place or to serve a counter notice requiring additional work to be done or to object to the work. If after 14 days your neighbour has not replied you will need to resolve the dispute before starting work.

## Resolving party wall issues

In the unlikely event that a dispute can't be resolved by friendly discussion, the Act provides for the resolution of disputes through a surveyor who will draw up a document that includes:

- A description of the work to be undertaken.
- When and how the work is to be carried out.
- A description of the condition of the neighbour's property prior to the work.
- Conditions allowing the surveyor access to inspect the work as it is carried out.

The surveyor will decide who pays the fee for drawing up the document, although it is up to the person undertaking the work to pay all costs.

## The right to light

In the case of any extension, neighbourhood Rights to Light can limit the height and position of the proposed building work and in certain cases actually reduce the site value. Rights to Light are difficult to track; they can be registered, granted by deed or simply acquired after having a minimum of 20 years enjoyment of light through a window or opening.

*The general rules for neighbours' Right to Light are:*

- *The reduction in light must make the property less fit than it was for its purpose.*
- *The amount of 'appropriate' light may vary depending upon building, use and even region.*
- *The amount of light considered to be sufficient will vary depending on the use of the room.*

# Design issues

Designing a conversion is a complex business. Both wiring and plumbing may have to be completely rethought to fit in with a new layout, for example, and this will be costly. Certain things, such as installing insulation, will be worth doing, but beware of fitting luxuries, such as a sauna, which may have only minority appeal. You certainly don't want to overdevelop and end up with a property that has cost you so much to revamp that you need to charge way over the local market value. Save your fantasies about games rooms for another day. The most common mistake made by vendors is a simple matter of failing to clean and clear any clutter from the property before showing it to potential buyers. Simple design and a good finish do not necessarily need to cost a fortune and this, together with a spotlessly clean property, is more important than throwing money away on fancy plans.

## Incorporating the services

The wiring, and especially the plumbing, can present real problems if you are going to alter the interior spaces of your property. The location of these services is crucial to the overall plan – for example, it will affect where the kitchen and bathroom should be located for greatest economy. At an early stage you should plot the existing power points, boilers, soil stacks and drainage runs on your plan. This should help you decide where the highly serviced rooms should be. There may be a choice of suitable positions. If not, adding extra foul drainage, for example, could prove costly.

## Jobs worth doing

It is always worth carrying out essential repairs to roofs and windows, and fitting sound wiring. Central heating and good insulation are also always worth installing. A well-painted front door with good quality door furniture, and a neat front garden are important, too. The key to getting it right is knowing your market and what prospective purchasers want.

Modernising a kitchen or bathroom is a good selling point but can be an expensive process. Installing a second bathroom is often a good idea, particularly if you are designing for a young family, but this also has the potential to be expensive.

*A well-designed central heating system that is beautifully fitted will not only run economically but is also a good selling point.*

If you buy a property with a good quality but tired kitchen, updating it without replacing it may take pressure off your budget, and a well-presented kitchen will always help when you come to sell. For example, wooden doors can be painted to freshen them up and new handles can be added to give a more contemporary look. Replacing a worktop can also make a dramatic difference. Paint walls and ceiling a clean neutral colour to brighten up the room. If your tiles look shabby, consider re-tiling, regrouting or scrubbing the grouting with bleach.

Don't forget the kitchen floor. Putting down good quality flooring in fairly neutral colours is often worth it as it will finish the whole room off.

# Period features

Period features, if they were fitted when the property was built, will not only fit its style but generally add to its value. Salvaging what you have can not only save you money but also appeal to your market. So think before you rip out any original features. If they are damaged, find out if they can be restored? Check what is waiting to be rediscovered beneath 'modern improvements'. The following are all items that would probably be worth keeping.

## Cornices
- If the original cornicing is damaged, you can hire a specialist to make a mould of a good part of it and repeat the pattern in plaster to replace the damaged area. You can replace the cornicing with a traditional standard moulding, but don't replace it with a cheap, mass-produced coving.

## Dado and picture rails
- Dado (or chair) rails were devised to prevent the backs of chairs from damaging the wall and are placed about 90cm (3ft) up the wall. They make an attractive visual break, particularly in rooms with high ceilings, and offer opportunities for using a combination of colours in the decoration.
- Picture rails are also decorative in their own right. FIxed to the wall about three-quarters of the way up, they were designed to hang pictures from.

## Fireplaces
- Even if it has central heating, in a period house a fireplace can act as a rather more attractive focal point than a television.
- Good stonemasons or marble restorers can restore chipped or broken surrounds (always get a quote). In general, wooden fire surrounds were originally painted. If you think yours would look better with a wood finish, the surround can be carefully stripped and treated.

- After alterations, if you end up with two fireplaces in a sitting room, but need one elsewhere, move the secondary one into a new position.

## Floors

- Exposing and restoring original flooring can add real value to a property. To revive hardwood floors give them a vigorous scrub with a mix of one part turpentine, one part methylated spirits and one part vinegar. Finish with floor polish.
- If pine or deal floorboards are worn you can sand them and finish with a sealant clear varnish. Beware, though, that sanding will remove the distinctive colour achieved by decades of wear.

## Doors

- If you want to make your period doors comply with fire regulations, use intumescent paint, which is fire-resistant, together with door closers, larger door stops and intumescent smoke seals.
- Victorian houses and some 1930s houses may still have original stained-glass surrounds to the front door. These can be very attractive.

## The bath

- Think before you rip out a tatty cast iron or roll-top bath sitting on decorative feet. The original is more desirable than modern plastic.
- A tatty bath can look like new again with either a professional polish or re-enamelling, and new taps.

## Shutters

- Keep original shutters as they are now seen as a valuable asset for both security and aesthetics (even if they need to be restored).

## Staircases

- The staircase will be very characteristic of the period of your house. If you alter an original staircase not only will you alter the proportions of the interior but your new staircase will have to comply with Building Regulations.

# Spatial solutions

Over half of Britain's housing stock was built before World War II, and the average living room is a mere 4.5 x 4m (15 x 13ft), but today's home-buyers are looking for as much space as they can get for their money. To make a limited area feel spacious you need good design. Even if you employ an architect or interior designer, it will help you to understand the spaces and possibilities if you sketch a floor plan. Go around the property with your sketch and review what you like about each room. Are they pleasing sizes and shapes? Do they connect up well? Then go around and list the least attractive elements of each room. Is it too dark? Is there an ugly view?

*You can't make a room physically larger without knocking down walls or building an extension, but you can make it feel bigger.*

### Using colour for a feeling of space
- Pale, light colours generally help to increase a sense of space. Shiny surfaces reflect light so consider using an eggshell or gloss paint (the shinier the surface the better the finish you need).

### Space-making floor treatments
- You can make a room with different areas (e.g. kitchen and dining area) feel larger if you change the covering in each area.
- Use hard, shiny coverings such as wood, resin, tile or slate in small spaces. These materials bounce light and sound, making the space feel larger.

### Ceilings
- Tall ceilings and smooth surfaces increase the sense of space. An artexed ceiling, for instance, will visually drip and will feel lower than it really is. Plaster and skim over Artex to push it back up.

## Make the most of light

- Daylight in a room gives it a sense of space. Add a window to a dark or small room or increase the scale of an existing one.
- Keep window treatments simple. Heavily draped curtains fill up visual space and cut down on light.
- Sight lines and views, especially of outside space, seem to visually expand our surroundings.

## Mirrors and pictures

- Use mirrors and pictures to reflect light. Place them strategically to reflect doors or paintings in a long narrow room or passage.
- If you have a low ceiling, place a large picture in the middle of the most dominant wall. This will draw your eye, detracting from the ceiling height.

## Stripes and lines

- The direction in which you lay a floor or patterned covering can have an impact. Vertical lines accentuate length, horizontal lines width.
- Wallpaper with vertical stripes draws the eye upwards and can increase the sense of height.

## Furniture

- Generally, only use furniture that is in proportion to the scale of the room.
- Moving furniture away from walls will reveal more wall space and make a room seem bigger.
- Less is more – the fewer things in a room the greater the feeling of space.

## Doors and doorways

- When completely renovating a period property, align doorways to create longer sight lines.
- Use sliding doors to maximise space, particularly those that disappear completely into cavity walls. Avoid cheap door systems.

## Storage

- Storage helps to keep spaces clutter-free. Use concealed storage with built-in cupboards.

## Humanising large spaces

Sometimes vast open spaces can feel much too large. They make us feel vulnerable and unable to relax. The answer is to visually cordon off sections of the room, using colour and furniture.

A rich, dark colour will add warmth to a large space but also tends to have the effect of bringing walls in. This can be particularly useful if you have a room with an irregular shape. A long, narrow room can appear squarer, for example, if you paint the furthest, smallest wall a dark colour to bring it closer to the eye. Strong colour on the long walls, on the other hand, will give a long, thin corridor effect. Use larger, more monumental pieces of furniture to zone specific areas within an over-large room.

# Major improvements

Altering the layout of a property can be a good idea if you can be sure that the end result will be a more satisfactory home. In most properties, while you may be able to make dramatic changes, this may not be best for your market. If there are large bedrooms but only one bathroom, consider creating an ensuite shower room in a corner of a bedroom. A cloakroom can often be tucked into spaces such as the cupboard under the stairs, depending on drainage. Roof space, with Building Regulations, can be used for anything from a study to a child's bedroom.

## Knocking through

It is usually possible to knock down a wall between two small rooms and create a larger one. You will need to comply with Building Regulations and also take advice from a structural engineer, who will calculate the size of any supporting beams required.

## Splitting up rooms

If the property has large rooms and you want to divide them, you will need some form of partition.

If you are merely building a stud wall to create two bedrooms out of one, or to separate a kitchen from a dining area, or a study from a living area, this is fairly straightforward and you can probably do it yourself. If you are creating two separate rooms out of one, you may need Building Regulation approval.

## Expanding into the loft

Lofts, even if the ceilings are low, can provide quite large rooms if well converted. It can be difficult to gain planning permission to raise the ridge height of the roof. Get into the roof space and work out whether you feel there is enough space and head height to justify the expense. Loft conversions are a way of adding extra square footage while only losing the area taken up by the new staircase.

Although they charge a premium, it can end up cheaper to get a specialist loft conversion company to carry out the work as they are geared up to tackle the specific work involved.

- Get two or three estimates, as these may vary considerably and check exactly what each covers, looking carefully at the clauses about insurance.
- Ask to see an example of the company's work.
- Agree everything in writing, including the size and frequency of the stage payments you will have to make.

If you are going to organise or even do the conversion yourself, you must take advice from an architect, surveyor and/or structural engineer. The work will have to comply with Building Regulations and may need planning permission. A professional will be able to advise about this.

**Regulations for loft conversions**  Because you are effectively adding another storey to your living space there are fire regulations to which you must adhere. This generally involves creating a route of escape down through the house that is protected against fire. This route cannot pass through another habitable room. You will need to either fireproof existing doors or install fire doors with self-closers along this route to meet the necessary regulations. A Fire Protection Officer or Building Regulations Officer will need to be satisfied that your changes comply with regulations.

*For a substantial extension you will require planning permission – smaller extensions may lie within your development rights.*

## Extending at ground level

Extending the property at ground level can make all the difference to the feeling of space. You may want just a few metres extra to fit in a porch for coats and boots, or a downstairs cloakroom. On a larger scale, you may want to build a full-scale conservatory with doors opening out onto the garden.

Whatever type of extension you want, there are a number of factors to take into account, and it really is best to get some expert advice.

- As a general rule, you will find it difficult to get approval to dramatically extend the roadside elevation or raise the ridge line of your house.
- Any proposed roof terrace is unlikely to be approved if it overlooks neighbouring gardens.
- Planning guidelines often change and you will need to check with your local council to keep up to date or employ an architect who will be familiar with the guidelines and help you come up with a proposal that is likely to be approved.
- The next thing is to complete an application form and prepare detailed drawings. An architect or surveyor is the best person to do this. They will also know about planning permission and Building Regulations and will apply for them on your behalf (see also pages 67–9).

## KEY**POINTS** FOR BUYING TO LET

*Before you embark on any renovation project,
you need to know who your market is and how
to target their needs accordingly. Refurnishing
a buy-to-let property is no different, but it does
have some particular requirements of its own.*

**For a more contemporary finish**, *if you are feeling
uninspired, hip hotels or trendy restaurants can really
help with ideas. The actual finishes and furnishings
might not be within your budget but you can borrow
ideas, look at the different materials and see how the
professionals put a look together.*

**At the more expensive** *end of the contemporary
market it is important to offer tenants luxurious
extras, but these don't have to cost a fortune. Start
with the basics – good, effective lighting is crucial,
as is making the space as user-friendly and flexible
as possible. Keep your colour palette limited and
apply different finishes rather than different colours.*

**Preparation is paramount.** *Before you invested
in a buy-to-let property you should already have
thought long and hard about the current use of
the property, its future prospects, as well as looked
at the amenities provided by the local area. You
will have determined which type of person these
particular attributes appeal to and researched how
much you are likely to achieve each month, to make
sure your investment is financially viable.*

**You will have checked** *that there is a demand for
rental property in the area, this is most important.
Now as you carry out refurbishment you need to
tailor the layout, style and facilities to fit that market.*

# Designing for rent

First of all you need to know your market. Think about what basic things your target tenant will want and expect from a rental property. A corporate client is likely to want all the gadgets and mod cons with a particularly high-spec finish. The student market, on the other hand, will opt for more basic budget accommodation and a simple decoration scheme.

*Make sure you have your potential purchaser clearly in mind and tailor the décor and furninshing to their tastes.*

Check that there is currently a demand for your type of property on the rental market. Look at similar homes available to rent in your area and seek advice from a letting agent. You should have already done this before you purchased the property, but if time has lapsed since you exchanged contracts, the market may have changed. You need to be up to date on current rental values so that you can budget for your design scheme accordingly. Planning carefully from the outset will keep you focused on your market and help you stick to your budget.

Whatever your market, design and spec, there are some general rules that will stand you in good stead when furnishing a buy-to-let.

## Décor

Keep your décor light and bright. As most tenants will only stay a year or so, you need to be able to appeal to a much broader market than for sale. (Any tenant will want a little leeway to add his or her own personality and taste, even if only for a short time.) For walls, stick to one colour throughout, preferably a neutral one. You will find this is easy to maintain and touch up between tenants, it is inoffensive to all and maximises the sense of light and space the property offers. Avoid loud colours and patterned papers, both of which rely on the tenant having the same taste as you.

## Flooring

Partly for ease of maintenance and partly to pull your scheme together, think about continuity. Laying the same flooring throughout, for example, helps the rooms to flow. Using different flooring will visually break up the space; in an open-plan space this can work to your benefit, giving the effect of two rooms whilst borrowing the extra space for a sight line.

Think carefully about the type of flooring you use.

- Carpet is an affordable option that appeals to most people. If you do choose carpet, avoid light colours as marks show more easily and it is best to go for a relatively cheap carpet that can be replaced every few years rather than spending a fortune on an expensive one that is likely to be damaged anyway.
- Solid wood and laminate floorings are easy to maintain and keep clean but whilst they are still popular at the moment, they may date fashion-wise in a relatively short period of time.
- Think twice about fitting wood flooring or carpet in bathrooms as they require the user to take a certain amount of care. You will find ceramic tiles or linoleum more durable and water resistant.

## Kitchen

Think practical and clean. If installing a new kitchen choose a simple, light-coloured modern design that is easy to maintain and keep clean. Buy affordable kitchen units that you can replace every few years. For worktops, avoid materials that damage, stain or burn easily such as wood, as tenants are less likely to take care of them. Make sure you install a splashback for the sink and cooking area to prevent walls getting greasy and grubby.

**HINTS&TIPS** PART OR FULLY FURNISHED

*Furnished and unfurnished properties generally command a similar rental price, but some areas and some properties will tend to let more easily unfurnished and vice versa. Do your research, get it right for your market and, if in doubt, consult a letting agent. Don't assume that you have to provide totally furnished accommodation. If the lease is for 6 or 12 months, part-furnished (fitted kitchen, bathroom, beds, sofas and table and chairs) is as much as the tenant is likely to want.*

1   *Think sturdy if you need to buy furniture.*

2   *If buying new tables and chairs go for simple and durable. Students and professionals will want a simple style – for a contemporary look buy copies of designer pieces that you can replace once they go out of fashion. Robust and grand antique pieces will look and wear perfectly in most period properties, especially in larger family units.*

3   *You may want to invest in one piece that sets off a room, such as a large mirror. It may be worth spending the extra money on this, depending on your market.*

4   *If you decide to let a property part-furnished, make sure you either have fitted wardrobes or provide freestanding ones.*

5   *If buying new beds, buy at the cheaper end of the market and replace them often. Mattresses will become marked before they wear out – replace them regularly regardless of whether they are worn out.*

Make sure all appliances are in full working order or replace them between tenants – leave a photocopy of the instructions and keep the originals in your filing system. Ideally, have a freestanding rather than integrated washing machine and fridge so that if anything goes wrong with either, you can slide it out easily for repairs or install a replacement.

## Bathroom

For bathrooms stick to a simple white suite and provide plenty of splashbacks. Most tenants like a good shower, so if you are able to fit one easily, do. If the room has a tired but perfectly good bathroom suite for your market, don't go to the expense of changing it. Think about scrubbing it up and just replacing the tiles, taps, a shower curtain and lavatory seat to give it all a fresh feel.

## Ventilation and extraction

Make sure all your rooms have adequate and efficient ventilation and extraction. This will help to prevent the build up of cooking smells and condensation and prevent damp and mould, especially in the bathroom.

## Furniture

Consider wear and tear when buying the furniture for a furnished property. Choose upholstery in dark colours to minimise staining and go for heavy fabric. Leather may sound like an expensive option but it has become much cheaper in recent years and it will get better and better with wear. You might also find a good piece second-hand, though again be aware that its style may be out of fashion before the piece wears out. Heavy canvas is another option. Washable loose covers are a good idea for chairs and sofas. You can also protect pieces with a proprietary stain repellent.

Note that as landlord, you are responsible for ensuring the upholstered furniture and soft furnishings you supply, whether new or second-hand (unless antiques), comply with the latest fire-resistance standards. The regulations apply to beds, mattresses, headboards, sofas, armchairs, and loose/stretch covers for furniture. They require that soft furniture has fire-resistant fillings and that fabric has passed appropriate match- or cigarette-resistance tests. You can obtain further information by contacting your local Trading Standards Office or the Department of Trade and Industry (DTI).

## Window dressings

You can buy very reasonable ready-made curtains or blinds – it is best to get a plain colour rather than a pattern as this appeals to all markets.

## Accessories

Do not be tempted to fill a rental flat with trinkets – accessories are for you own home, not a rental flat. The tenants will want to surround themselves with their own possessions, not yours.

# Making the most of professionals

As a first-time developer you cannot possibly expect to have all the skills needed to see the whole project through to a successful conclusion, so it's important to know when to call in the professionals. You should certainly employ an architect if you intend to carry out any major architectural or structural changes to your property. They will tell you whether what you are proposing is possible and how to achieve it, and will advise on the best approach for your particular property and your purse strings. They will also advise on how to achieve more light, space or rooms in your property. While the results can be wonderful, their skills, of course, come at a cost.

If you are making structural changes you will need the services of a surveyor. For insurance reasons, a structural surveyor will generally need to be employed directly by you although they will also work closely with your architect, project manager and builder.

Before starting out, make sure that the proposed architectural/structural changes will increase the market value of your property by an amount that covers the cost of the work and provides you with an additional profit for your efforts.

To find an architect seek advice from the RIBA (Royal Institute of British Architects).

---

## ✓ CHECK**LIST** PLANNING

1  *Assess the extent of work required to make the house right for your market, taking note of all the things mentioned in the building survey.*

2  *Make sure you comply with Building Regulations and that you get any necessary planning permissions. Do this as early as possible – consent may take some weeks to come through.*

3  *Alienated neighbours can be very obstructive. See that you are on good terms with them.*

4  *Make sure your design will not be so expensive that it gobbles up all your potential profit.*

5  *Make the most of period features. Don't rip everything out without a thought as many items will be an added attraction for potential buyers.*

6  *Tailor the property to your market and if you are buying to let, remember that this market has particular requirements of its own.*

7  *Find a reputable architect and/or builder. Discuss the project with them before you appoint them and choose the one you think will understand what you want; don't necessarily go for the cheapest.*

# 5 project management

Managing the restoration or conversion of any building is an extraordinarily complex business. It is vital to set up a workmanlike environment from which the whole project can be efficiently directed. You need to be disciplined and orderly, good with figures, good with people, good at juggling priorities, dates and order of work, and at keeping within budget. If you do not feel up to this, employing an efficient manager will save money in the long run.

# Managing your development

The success of a development is partly dependent on a smooth running site. Whether you choose to develop one property at a time, or several concurrently, do some careful planning to ensure that your site(s) stays on schedule. The first decision you should make is whether to oversee the work yourself or to employ an experienced project manager. On a larger site you really need a site manager who is on hand every day. On a job where you are subcontracting work to a number of different tradesmen such as joiners, plumbers, electricians and decorators, it can be difficult to co-ordinate their activities and ensure that the work progresses smoothly. Depending on your experience and the time you are able to devote to the project, paying someone to do either or both jobs for you will help avoid the project grinding to a halt. It is still important, however, that you keep in touch with what's going on from day to day.

**The building contract**  If you are paying someone else to run a job for you it is wise to have a contract (for example in line with the JCT Agreement for Minor Building Works 1998 Edition) drawn up for the whole project. One possibility is to download a free, ready-made contract at the Federation of Master Builders website (www.fmb.org.uk).

**The project manager**  As well as having lots of time, energy and the right contacts, a project manager needs to run the site like a military operation, as well as developing a good working relationship with everyone involved. A happy team means you are more likely to get good results and swift work, which will get you nearer your profit faster.

**How much time can you spend on-site?**  Ask yourself whether you have all the necessary skills, as well as the time and money to be your own project manager. If you are committed to another full-time job, then the answer is most probably 'no'. If your working hours are flexible then you must think of project managing one site as a full-time job, no less. In my experience, you will not be able to work elsewhere for a large chunk of the day and simultaneously fit in working on-site, overseeing labour and ordering materials into 24 hours.

**Can you afford to give up the day job?**  It is essential you are realistic about how much profit you need to make a year to provide yourself with an income before you think about developing full-time and giving up the day job. The workload associated with this role means that project managers usually command a payment of at least 10%, if not 20%, of the value of the project. To save this money, many first-time developers try to oversee the project themselves. However, inexperience can result in

## HINTS&TIPS PROJECT MANAGING

*Project managing is one of the most important roles on-site. The responsibilities of a project manager include:*

**Running** *the site from the beginning to the end of the project.*

**Ensuring** *that the site complies with legal requirements.*

**Ensuring** *the site is safe.*

**Hiring** *all the sub-contractors and tradesmen needed for the job.*

**Scheduling** *their works in sequential order and making sure the work is carried out within the budget and time-scale agreed with the owner of the property.*

**Paying** *the sub-contractors' wages and complying with current subcontractor tax regulations.*

**Ordering** *all the materials required.*

**Arranging** *for the supplies to arrive at the right time.*

**Making** *big decisions, but also clearing up the site and ensuring tea, coffee and loos are available.*

**Usually** *being on-site approximately six days a week for several hours, arriving around 7.00 am. The project manager is inevitably the person putting in the extra labour if things run behind schedule.*

hiccups and a lack of planning early on or even partway through can cause overruns in budget and schedule, which can have costly consequences. Take a long look at your salary. If you can afford to pay a project manager, then question why you shouldn't.

If the building work you plan to have done is relatively minor (lasting just a few days) you should at least draw up a very basic contract between you and the builder.

*While there's a lot to be said for employing a manager, if you are up to the challenge of the day-to-day running of a project, and are committed to doing it yourself, here are some tips to help you get off to a good start.*

- *Get your site organised as soon as contracts are exchanged. Source your materials and find the right contractors/tradesmen as swiftly as possible.*

- *Have back-up tradesmen and builders on standby. Ask friends or fellow-developers for recommendations. Keep a database of contact details and start to build up good contacts.*

- *Using your schedule of works, draw up a chart of what works need to happen on-site and when. Order materials at the right time. Too much too early will result in a cluttered site, a security risk, and you will find that you have to constantly shift heavy items from room to room so tradesmen can do their work. It also increases the risk of goods being damaged. Too much too late means that jobs come to a standstill and your schedule slides. If materials are coming from overseas check that the shipping time fits with your schedule. Consider using self-storage.*

- *Be crystal clear with all tradesmen. Always work out exactly what you want done before you request a quote for a job, however small. Draw a plan and write down instructions – give a copy to the sub-contractor, keep one for yourself and file the originals. Many problems with craftsmen are due to vague or incomplete initial instructions.*

- *Control your sub-contractor's costs. Always negotiate fees upfront and stick to a written agreement, unless unforeseen circumstances arise and you change the work that needs to be done – in which case be fair and agree on an extra payment.*

- *Keep on top of all the work that happens on-site so that you can be sure you are happy with the quality of the work. Always pay contractors on time but make sure you are happy with the results of their labour before doing so.*

- *Be organised with your paperwork, and keep a constant eye on your budget.*

- *Be realistic about your capabilities. If you are new to developing, don't dabble in complicated building processes or difficult features.*

**Managing more than one project** *If you have built up some property developing experience and several suitable ventures become available, you may decide to develop more than one property at once. Here are some tips for keeping things running smoothly when you can't be in several places at once.*

- *Think carefully before you take on multiple projects. Get financial advice and don't overstretch yourself. Think about what will happen if both sites do not sell/rent. Cash-flow is key.*

- *Employ a very capable site manager on each site to keep things running smoothly.*

- *Keep on top of paperwork and budgets. If you don't know what you have spent on which site, you don't know whether it will make a profit.*

- *Avoid robbing Peter to pay Paul. If one site is running over budget, don't be tempted to steal funds from another to make up the difference.*

- *There are positive implications with running several sites. Consider bulk buying, for example. You can negotiate better discounts if you buy a large quantity of materials at the same time.*

- *If you come across a problem, stop and think logically before you act upon it, even when time is key. It is always costly to go back on a decision.*

# Schedule of works

Plan out everything on a big wall chart. In addition, make lists of the work to be done and details for each job, including when you have employed contractors and when you expect deliveries to arrive. Make sure that things happen at the right time; doing so means that you won't book in the plasterer before the electrician is finished or the kitchen fitter before the units arrive. Every extra day on the schedule puts a strain on your budget.

## Order of work

This list of work to be done will help you plan your own project. You can tailor it to suit your own needs.

### Preparation
- Clear furniture, carpets, etc.
- Protect other areas from dust and debris.

### Demolition
- Make sure floors, partitions and walls are correctly supported where load-bearing sections are to be altered or removed.
- Demolish unwanted structures; strip redundant and disconnected plumbing, electrics, fittings and finishes, and remove rubbish.

### Special treatments
Each of the following jobs can be done by specialist contractors who will provide guarantees against work carried out that can be passed onto your buyer.
- Hack off plasterwork to a metre high in the areas requiring remedial work for rising damp.
- Install damp-proof course.
- Lift floorboards and carry out timber treatment if necessary (to stop or prevent woodworm).
- Expose any dry rot and cut back all timber past the affected area by recommended amounts before the area is sprayed.
- Sweep chimneys and flues and reline if required.

## Basic construction/Adding services

- Lay the groundwork for drains, foundations and incoming services.
- Water, gas, electricity and telephone supplies.

## Building

- Build new brickwork of any extension (incorporating new damp-proof course) with lintels, door and window frames, making provision for external meters, extractors, waste pipes, etc.
- Repointing brickwork (including chimneys), or hacking off and re-rendering external walls.
- Pour ground floor slab ensuring correct damp-proof membrane and insulation are used.
- Fill in after groundwork around building.
- Erect any new internal walls (including insulation).
- Replace timberwork as required.
- Carry out any required replastering.
- Joinery as required.

## Water/plumbing

- Mains supply to be fitted to the property.
- Run pipework for hot and cold supply to kitchen, bathrooms, outside tap as required.
- Run pipework to all radiator points.

---

**KEYPOINTS** HEALTH AND SAFETY

*There are strict* Health and Safety regulations that must be complied with under the Health and Safety at Work Act of 1974 which applies to any place where a work activity is undertaken. Many will apply to your site. You should either ring the Information Line on 08701 545500 to ask for advice or visit their website on www.hse.gov.uk where you can find free leaflets that can be printed out on the health and safety requirements for all sorts of areas of construction and employment.

- Install hot and cold water storage tanks.
- Install and connect boiler (if gas, must be done by a CORGI-registered plumber).
- Carcass out bathroom and kitchen in preparation for installation of fixtures.
- Run waste from bathrooms and kitchen.
- Install bathroom fittings and connect.
- Second fix kitchen once it is fitted.

**Gas/electricity/telephone**
- Run all pipework required for gas fires, boiler, oven and hob as required.
- First fix all wiring (run all cables without connecting up to supply).
- Second fix wiring (fit all light fittings, switches and sockets, test circuits and connect to the supply).
- Fit new consumer unit if required.
- Fit alarm (if suitable).

**Floors and roofing**
- Re-roof or build new roof structure where required, install insulation.
- Fit soil, vent and rainwater pipes, and gutters.

**Finishing: first finishes**
- Decoration, tiling, door and window furniture to be fitted, skirting/architrave to be fitted, cornicing where required, floor tiling/finishes to be laid.

**Fitting out**
- Installation of kitchen and bathroom units, wardrobes, cupboards, baths, showers, loos, radiators, cookers and other appliances.

**Decoration**
- Preparation: sand and fill, hang lining paper where required, prime and undercoat.
- Final finishes: paint colours and wall coverings.

**External works**
- Clear site of debris.
- Hard and soft landscaping.

# Who does what?

Unless you are trained or very experienced it makes sense to employ an architect and a main contractor to organise and oversee any major or structural work. And it probably makes sense to get professionals to do the majority of the rest of the work. If you are reasonably well organised and practically minded, you could do some of the minor work yourself, such as stripping out and basic joinery. But it is most unwise to attempt to replace a roof or move a staircase without any experience. You may consider it too expensive to employ others but in the long run it would be better to modify your plans than to embark on major works yourself and end up unable to complete the job, or worse, hurting yourself.

> *Make sure that you choose people who are skilled, experienced and competent in the particular job you want them to do.*

However, if you're confident enough to tackle any electrical or plumbing work, it is essential that you are very careful and that you have it checked by a professional – all gas work needs to be carried out by a CORGI-registered plumber and new kitchens and bathrooms need to comply with local Building Regulations. A mistake in the wiring can cause a fatal accident with electrocution or a fire.

## Finding a builder

Choosing a good builder is essential to the smooth and swift running of any development. The best way to source a good builder is to get a referral from family and friends who have recently had similar work done. Otherwise check with a trade association such as the National Federation of Builders (NFB), which can advise you on how to source a reputable, quality tradesman. The NFB has membership criteria covering workmanship, financial status, and health and safety, and also operates a Code of Practice to try to help safeguard customers. Its members are encouraged to provide references from customers, suppliers and financial institutions. No guarantee of workmanship is given, but it is better than opening the Yellow Pages. There have been cases of builders fraudulently claiming membership of official trade associations, so check they are bona fide members.

Ask three builders to quote for the job:

- Prepare a detailed schedule of works you want done throughout the property. Include drawings where necessary, be specific and give as much detail as possible. Give a copy to each builder and ask them to give you a quotation.
- Encourage each builder to submit an itemised quote for the project. From this you will be able to see where and how to reduce costs – maybe by deciding to do more of the project yourself. You can try haggling, but be aware that if you force the price down too far, you may come unstuck at some point in the project as there is no reason why he should work on your project for nothing. The harsh reality is that the only way to reduce costs is to do less work.

If one of the three quotes is dramatically less than the others be cautious about automatically going with it – ask your architect or surveyor why they vary so much. Check them over to see if there are major differences in what they are planning to do. A builder who gives a very low quotation may well realise halfway through that it was an unrealistic figure, leaving him with no profit – this is where problems will start to set in and it may even end up with them leaving the job unfinished.

While accepting a higher quotation does not guarantee that work will be completed within a specified time, if the contractor has a healthier profit margin, he is more likely to be on your job than another. Ensure that you are given a quotation not just an estimate before a builder begins work. An estimate is an approximate guide to what you can expect to pay, whereas once he has given you a quotation for the work this is the amount that a contractor is expecting to be paid for the job. Insist that the builder provides a written quotation and signs your contract. For major works, ensure that the contract states when payments should be made.

## Paying the builder

On small contracts, lasting less than four or five weeks, most builders will not expect payment until work is completed. On bigger jobs it is usual to pay agreed percentages of the total cost at specified stages of the work. Some estimates will include 'provisional sums'. These are normally used for work the builder has to sub-contract and has not obtained firm estimates for. Make sure you are consulted before a provisional sum becomes a firm price.

**Finding a plumber**  Plumbers need to be supplied with a detailed specification indicating which fixtures are to go where. Get at least two or three estimates and try to use firms that have been recommended to you by people who have used them. Alternatively, contact the Institute of Plumbing who can give you

---

 KEY**POINTS** INSURANCE FOR BUILDERS

*When having work* done on your property check to see if the contractor has public liability insurance. This will pay for any negligence on their part that results in property damage or injury to you or your colleagues. Legally they do not have to have this insurance, but it is sensible for them to have it. If a long leasehold tenant is carrying out any building work, a landlord may ask for insurance. But for a freeholder it is a personal choice. It is advisable for cases of poor workmanship, for accidents, not to mention third party liability (if scaffolding collapsed, causing injury).

the names of registered plumbers in your area. All members are encouraged to adhere to the Institute's Code of Professional Standards.

**Finding a gas fitter**  CORGI (The Confederation for the Registration of Gas Installers) is the watchdog for gas safety in th UK and the leading authority on gas safety issues. It provides members of the public with details of locally registered gas fitters.

**Finding a glazier**  The Glass and Glazing Federation is a trade association and an authority on flat glass, glazing, window and home improvement plastics. Members work to a Code of Good Practice and to the Federation's technical standards. It will give advice on glass, and names of local members.

**Finding an electrician**  Use a professional; all work must comply with local codes. The Institute of Electrical Engineers is the main body regulating codes of practice and if you use a member you will have recourse to the institute should anything go wrong. The Electrical Contractors Association encourages its members to provide high quality, good value and safe installation.

**HINTS&TIPS** CONTINGENCIES

*Earmark part of your budget for contingencies. The sort of things that may cause problems are:*

**Altering the specification** *or anything in the contract you have agreed with the builder.*

**Delay in getting permissions** *such as Building Regulations approval or Party Wall Agreements.*

**Delays in deliveries** *of materials/equipment which means work cannot go ahead as quickly as planned.*

**Extra expenses** *incurred through having to hire equipment (such as scaffolding) or doing work (such as repairing the roof) that you had not foreseen.*

# Finishing the project

For many, especially first-time developers, the final decorating is the most interesting and exciting part of the whole project. But remember, just as you planned the interior spaces for your target market and not for yourself, you should also be decorating for your target market. Be clear about who you have decided to sell to, but at the same time don't be too specific. Every buyer wants to put his or her own personality into their home. So you should provide them with a beautifully designed blank canvas on which they can do this. At the same time, don't discard all the period features (see pages 74–5) – try to retain the character of the original building.

**Glass**  Natural and artificial light can be enhanced by glass in many ways. Glass bricks built into a wall can lighten up a dark basement surprisingly well.

**Stained glass panels**  These glass panels were used in and to surround front doors in Victorian houses and some 1930s homes. This type of glass is generally thinner than much of the glass used today (3–4mm) and there is often concern over security. To make it more secure you can back the glass with toughened burglar-proof translucent plastic.

**Wood**  A traditional house will often have lots of wooden surfaces, from floorboards to fireplace surrounds. It is usually wise to keep as much as you can of the original wood, which will be sympathetic to the design and date of the building.

   If you have to remove some of the wood, replace it with wood that, even if not exactly the same will still be in keeping with the house.

**Window shutters**  Internal wooden shutters can still be found in some of the larger Victorian houses. Apart from being attractive in their own right, they act as another form of insulation.

**Wood panelling**  Wood panelling is one of the most attractive finishes for a wall and was used in traditional homes, partly to act as insulation and partly to show off the beauty of particular woods. Manufacturing developments have made this a fairly inexpensive finish – large areas can be covered in veneered plywood sheets which come with a variety of surfaces. The best quality have a real wood veneer.

Alternatively tongue-and-groove boards (also known as matchboarding) are usually made of white wood or knotty pine. They are very suitable for small Victorian homes, in bedrooms and bathrooms.

*The final stage of your property development – finishing off – may seem easy. But it's important to get this cosmetic part right or you may put potential buyers off.*

**Wooden floors**  Wood has been used for centuries to create attractive floors. Parquet flooring would hardly be cost-effective in most houses. Solid wooden boards are available, but they may not be cost-effective for the developer. But you can sand and seal old floorboards or replace old boards with a wood block or wood strip floor, available in various woods and very easy to lay.

**Plaster and decorative mouldings**  Decorative plasterwork can be a good indication of the age and importance of a house. During the 1960s many mouldings were ripped out or hidden behind partition walls and suspended ceilings, but the current popularity of classically proportioned walls means there are now plenty of choices for replacing mouldings, from traditional designs to modern ones.

**Friezes, cornices and ceiling roses**  Plaster cornices can be cast to match specific designs and are expensive, but there are good standard designs available at a reasonable cost. Avoid resorting to coving in a Victorian house – it would not have originally been used. Keep decorative plasterwork in proportion with the house.

**Wallpapers: Anaglypta and Lincrusta**  Victorian wallpaper producers developed imitation panelling and moulding in embossed papers which were sold under the trade names Lincrusta and Anaglypta. These almost completely replaced wall plasterwork. Similar but lighter and more pliable embossed Lincrusta and Anaglypta papers are available today to give an original look to Victorian houses.

In many unrestored Victorian houses, layers of original wallpaper can still be found. Reproductions of these old styles are available today so it is relatively easy to reproduce the look, especially if you have some original paper as a model.

**Ceramic tiles**  Ceramic tiles are durable and many have survived since Victorian times. They can be found on fireplace surrounds and in bathrooms. You can get modern reproductions of Victorian tiles, inspired by the designs of the time so it is not difficult to replace any damaged areas. Some damage can be acceptable to old tiles and adds to the period feel, whereas new tiles if not of the same quality can often detract from the overall effect.

**Radiators and screens**  Original Victorian cast-iron radiators are now difficult to find and are not always very efficient. But there are companies producing efficient and modern look-alikes of the originals.

Radiator screens were used by the Victorians to hide the massive heating contraptions in many large houses. You can get copies of these, often in MDF.

**The bathroom**  If you find a roll-top bath in the property you buy, consider making the most of it by cleaning it up and creating a Victorian bathroom.

There are faithful reproductions of traditional baths, basins, lavatory bowls and cisterns as well as fittings such as taps and showerheads.

# Gardens

Many people embarking on property development dismiss the garden as an unimportant detail. This is a big mistake. Gardens can make or break a potential sale. If a front garden looks drab it will immediately colour the viewer's impression of the whole property.

The garden is one of the main attractions for many people, not only retired people and young families but also young couples who see it as an extra space in which to entertain and socialise. So it is important not to fit it in as an afterthought.

## Walls and fences

- Planning permission is needed if you want to build a fence or wall 1m (3ft) high next to a public highway or footpath, or on other boundaries if the fence is over 2m (6ft) high. Always contact your local planning authority before erecting a fence or wall.
- Do not be tempted to put a deterrent (barbed wire) on top of a wall. If this causes a nuisance or, by your negligence, injures a passer-by, then they may be able to sue you for damages.
- Do not build a wall or fence, without permission, on a neighbour's land – this is legal trespass. Your neighbour can obtain a court injunction telling you to remove the wall and sue you for damages.

## Trees and shrubs

- A tree or shrub belongs to the owner of the land it grows on, even if its branches or roots go over or under adjoining land. You are not allowed to go onto your neighbour's land or to lean over it to cut your hedge without his/her permission. If falling leaves from your tree block a neighbour's gutter, you could be liable for any water damage.
- Branches that overhang your neighbour's land are trespassing on their air space. The neighbour can chop the branches back to the boundary (beyond the boundary is trespass) but must return the

lopped branches to you. It's always best to discuss the matter with your neighbour first.

- The local authority can make a tree preservation order to prohibit felling or lopping certain trees. You can be fined up to £20,000 for ignoring this. Trees in a Conservation Area have strict regulations protecting them. Always check with the local authority before getting rid of a tree.

- Roots can often lead to substantial damage by growing under the foundations of a building and sucking up all the moisture in the ground. If your tree roots cause damage to a neighbour's house you could be liable for the cost of repairs, and other expenses.

---

### 💡 HINTS&TIPS CREATING A GARDEN PLAN

*A garden provides greenery, privacy, somewhere pleasant to sit or to entertain, a space for children to play, shade on a hot day and extra useful space. Do not underestimate its importance.*

- *Measure the space and draw a rough plan that includes the doors to the house and windows looking out onto the garden. Sketch in the sort of garden that will appeal to your target market.*

- *A pond is not a good idea if you are thinking of selling or renting to families with young children. Similarly, affluent business types may not appreciate masses of lawn, preferring instead the convenience of a low-maintenance surface.*

- *A patio area at one end will be necessary and you can add other seating areas elsewhere in the garden to catch the sun at different times of day.*

- *Why not add a fountain or other water feature, or perhaps a barbecue and a bed for herbs near the kitchen door?*

# Presenting to sell

After months of research, planning, careful budgeting and serious amounts of hard work, you will be itching to know whether all your efforts have paid off financially. In short, you want a sale. You will, however, still need to make an effort! This is the final phase in the development, but it is an important one.

Use my three-stage strategy to get things looking great before you book in any valuations:
- First impressions/outside appearances are crucial.
- If it doesn't move, clean it!
- Suggest a lifestyle for living in the space.

## Outside appearances

If you have a front garden, the finishing touches should be to mow the lawn, sweep the paths and get rid of any weeds and litter. Also, make sure the skip will be collected in good time and that any dustbins are emptied and tidied away. If your neighbours have left a pile of rubbish on view, offer to remove it. Your aim is to create a good first impression of a well-maintained and tidy home.

Does the front door need painting or need new door furniture? This is your last chance to remedy things if the entrance looks dull. Next, get all of the windows cleaned, inside and out. It makes a massive difference to be able to see out from the inside, as well as the difference more light makes to the interior.

## If it doesn't move, clean it!

Try to set aside at least a whole day for cleaning, unless you choose to call in a professional cleaning company. Invest in two pairs of industrial-strength gloves, lots of cleaning products, new dusters, sponges, tea towels and any specialist products you may need such as fluid for polishing stainless steel. Remember to bring the vacuum, a mop, bucket, and dustpan and brush from home.

## 🔑 HINTS&TIPS CLEANING SCHEDULE

1   *Start at the top of the house and clean each room from top to bottom, literally!*

2   *Remove any rubbish or leftover tools, then start by cleaning the highest surfaces, such as the tops of wardrobes and light fittings.*

3   *Wipe over furniture, shelving, door frames and window ledges with a damp cloth to remove layers of building dust and dirt before dusting.*

4   *Clean and polish any pieces of furniture and vacuum upholstered furniture.*

5   *Polish door handles, mirrors and pictures and other fixtures such as light fittings.*

6   *Check that there are no signs of any paint on the light switches/sockets, door or window furniture. Scrape off any excess paint and wipe them over.*

7   *Use a damp cloth to clean inside any cupboards, cabinets or wardrobes. Viewers do open these.*

8   *Check that all lights are fitted with working bulbs. Many professionals choose to view properties after work, in fading light.*

9   *Make sure your bathroom suite is immaculate. Scrub and shine up your bath, basin, shower and loo, inside and out. Polish taps and mirrors.*

10  *In the kitchen, make sure the oven, hob, fridge and washing machine are all clean and sparkling. Work surfaces should be spotless, taps and door handles should shine. Wipe down cupboards inside and out.*

11  *Dust all the skirting boards and radiators.*

12  *Vacuum all of the carpets and rugs, as well as other flooring (polished/painted wooden floors, tiled or vinyl floors) to get rid of building dust before mopping them with suitable cleaner. Don't forget the stairs.*

# Managing a buy-to-let

To develop property, you need to successfully juggle a myriad of roles. If you decide to buy to let, you will need to add 'landlord' to your repertoire of skills. Knowing what to charge for rent is important. Look on the Internet and in letting agents' brochures to see the rental prices of similar properties.

**Becoming a landlord**  Depending on your situation, you may choose to go it alone – manage all aspects of the property yourself – or to employ a letting agent, who will be able to provide one of the following four options. (These come at a cost; commission is based on the monthly rental income.)

- Introduction service: The agent simply finds you a tenant – approximate commission is 10%.
- Introduction and rent collection: In addition, the agent administers monthly rent collection – approximate commission is 12.5%.
- Full management service: In addition, the agent manages the property, including any repairs – approximate commission is 15%.
- Full management service plus rental guarantee: In addition, the agent guarantees a percentage of the rent – approximate commission is 17%.

## Finding a good managing agent

Visit three local agencies, with a clear idea of the role you wish them to take on. Then ask them the following questions:

- How do they market the lets in their area? This will give you an indication of their profile.
- How many tenants do they have on their books?
- Do they belong to any of the national letting agents' organisations such as ARLA (Association of Residential Letting Agents) or NAEA (National Association of Estate Agents). These agencies offer support and guidance should you happen to fall into dispute with one of their member agents.
- Do they have professional indemnity insurance?

In addition, ask them for a list of their services and fees so you know exactly what you will be getting for your money. Check that the agent is able to provide you with a signed tenancy agreement, inventory, references, employer's contact details, and at least one month's deposit and one month's rent in advance from a future tenant. Lastly, insist that rent is paid by standing order, straight into your bank account.

If you decide to hire a letting agent you will need to organise a valuation. Set up three valuations with different companies. Your gross rent should be at least between 130–150% of your monthly loan repayments. Your net rental income should cover mortgage costs and management fees and leave you with sufficient profit to make the project viable. Remember that this profit will probably be called upon to cover costs of repairs or vacant periods.

 KEY**POINTS** A LANDLORD'S DUTIES

*Whether you employ a letting agent or not, there are still some responsibilities which you, as a landlord, will need to undertake by law.*

1   *You will need a certificate to prove that any gas appliances and gas boilers are safe.*

2   *You will need to ensure that there are adequate fire escapes and fire extinguishers and that you meet all fire regulations. Check with your council.*

3   *All soft furnishings and upholstered furniture must comply with fire regulations and be made from non-flammable materials.*

4   *You will need buildings insurance. Add clauses which protect the tenant against injury on the premises as well as protecting the property from any malicious damage.*

5   *Employ an electrician to service any electrical appliances. This is not currently mandatory, changes are anticipated in the near future.*

# Self-managing a rental property

If you manage a property yourself, don't be tempted to let it to people you know. This can complicate the tenant/landlord relationship and contribute to problems, such as late payment of rent. Keep on top of repairs so that the property does not deteriorate.

If you are tempted to go it alone, you are advised to do all of the following:

- Do some serious research into the rental market in your area. Be realistic when deciding on a monthly figure – neither price yourself out of the market nor fall short of the market value.

- Have an Assured Shorthold Tenancy Agreement drawn up. This is a legally binding document designed to protect both the landlord and the tenant. You can buy a ready-made contract or ask your solicitor to draft the agreement for you.

- Whether you are letting an unfurnished, part- or fully-furnished property, get an impartial expert to draw up a legally binding inventory for you and your tenant. This will give you, as landlord, the right to hold back part or all of a deposit if any items are damaged during the tenant's stay.

- Build up a contacts database, via personal recommendations, so that you have reliable tradesmen that you can call upon in the event of something going wrong.

- Insist your tenants pay you by standing order. These are easy to set up between banks and will minimise the hassle of having to chase rent.

- Keep handy a note of tenants' contact details.

- Leave a list of useful contact details in the rental property so that tenants can easily contact service providers and the council without calling you first. It is essential to include your own details.

- Leave instructions for operating such things as the central heating, hot water and electric shower, together with any relevant guarantees.

- Keep at least two spare sets of keys yourself so that you can lend them out to contractors or to tenants if they mislay theirs or lock themselves out. Make sure you retain the master set.

- Make appointments to inspect the property every now and then with your tenant. Get someone to fix the little jobs that you notice when you visit, so that these problems don't escalate. And have the boiler serviced regularly so that it is less likely to let you down. Your tenant reserves the right to disallow you entry to the property unless you make a prior arrangement to visit them.

Remember, the more properties you own that are let, the more hassle you will have for your money. Think carefully about whether this is really something you want to do and if you are motivated enough to make this type of venture happen.

---

##  CHECK**LIST** ON THE JOB

**Make sure** you have an efficient site and project manager. If you are going to do the managing yourself, make sure you understand what's involved and that you have the necessary skills and the time.

**Draw up** a schedule of works so that everything is done in the right order and on time. Keep a chart of the progress of the development. Find out where to source good quality materials at a good price.

**Make sure** that whoever is doing the work is experienced and skilled. For electrical, plumbing and gas work it is essential to use a professional.

**Always plan** for contingencies. Something unforeseen is bound to come up at some stage.

**When finishing** the project, make the décor and furnishings simple. Keep your target market in mind. Make the most of period features; don't over-furnish.

**Don't forget** the garden. This is one of the main attractions for many people so tackle it seriously.

**If you want** to let the property, find out all you can about managing a property or employ a good managing agent. Check on the responsibilities you will have as a landlord.

# 6 selling a property

Selling might be the final step in the property development ladder, but it's one you should consider from the start. It will be the final test of whether your development has been successful and profitable and the potential resale value of the property will govern how much and what type of development you undertake. As with all aspects of property ownership, selling a house is complicated. Find out what the realistic asking price is for homes in the area and don't go too far above it, particularly if there are a lot of similar properties for sale.

# Getting a valuation

Ideally, you should look for three reputable agents based in your area to give you a valuation. If you bought the property from an estate agent and were happy with their services, then they are a good place to start. To find two others, look at the companies most actively marketing similar homes for sale in your area. Does the estate agent have regular advertisements in the local press, an easy-to-use website with links to property portals and lots of 'sold' or 'for sale' boards dotted around your neighbouring streets? These are all good signs.

To save on time, book in staggered appointments for all your agents to view the property on the same day. Ask the agents to bring along details of properties they have recently sold that are similar in size and style to yours. The prices that these homes actually sold for will give you a good indication of the current market. But before you make those appointments, do your research:

- Look at the local property press, agents' websites and property details through the eyes of a buyer.
- Check the sale prices of properties similar to your own. Get a feel for the market – it may have changed since you bought the property.
- See how many properties like yours are for sale. If there is a glut of such properties, you will need to be even more realistic about your asking price, unless you are offering something extra.

A common mistake made by home-owners when selling is to be flattered by the highest valuation they receive and to choose that agent. The reality is that a house is worth only what a purchaser will pay for it, and remember that an estate agent is not a buyer. If you have done your research you should be able to spot an inflated valuation.

# Estate agents

You've seen three estate agents – now you need to decide which one to market your property with. Do you choose one or several agents? If you sign a sole agency agreement with more than one estate agent, you may be legally obliged to pay fees twice.

Once you have chosen an agent, build up a good rapport with them. As with any relationship, if estate agents like and respect you, they will do more to help sell your property. To get the most out of the agent-vendor relationship, consider the following:

- Commission: In theory an estate agent's commission fee is negotiable. However, don't haggle over 0.5% or 1%. It will make little difference to your gross profit and could scupper your relationship.
- Negotiate a contract: Put your property on with an agent for the minimum contract time – usually

four weeks. During this period the agent will have an influx of viewers lined up from their existing database. If you are pleased with the service and the number of viewings, extend the contract.

- Marketing details: The agent will compile written details and take photographs of the property for marketing. Make sure you are happy with the photographs they plan to use. A bad picture could put off home-hunters from booking a viewing. Check that the right descriptions and measurements of the rooms appear; that the best features are mentioned, as well as sought-after extras such as the garden, parking and the proximity to travel links and amenities.

*Estate agents are legally obliged to give correct and accurate details of the property. Mistakes do happen, however, so do check the details yourself.*

- Viewings: Let the estate agent conduct the viewings. This will allow the home-hunter to feel comfortable and be objective.
- Communications: Arrange a time each week when you and your agent can discuss the viewings that have taken place. Ask for any feedback and the number of parties that they have shown around the property. Note the feedback (including any negative criticism) and, if necessary, think about how you could redress the problem, or drop the price accordingly.
- Building work and guarantees: Keep information about any work you have had carried out in a box file, including any certificates for works, building regulation and planning permission certificates. Send copies of these to your estate agent and also to your solicitor in preparation for a sale.
- Also keep handy guarantees for any appliances, any service history for a boiler and the manual for how to work the central heating system.

## Solicitors

A good solicitor or licensed conveyancer for your sale is crucial. If you were satisfied with the one you used for the purchase of the property, there will be no problem. If not, you will need to find one you can rely on and fast. (See pages 53–6, for information on finding a solicitor and their responsibilities).

Remember to ask the solicitor for a breakdown of the conveyancing fees before you give them the go ahead to do any work on your behalf. Find out whether they provide a 'no move, no fee' service – it could save you a lot of money. Do not always be cost-driven with a solicitor; remember, as with most things you will often get what you pay for.

## Selling privately

This is another possible option, but in my opinion the pitfalls outweigh the benefits and so I would rarely recommend you plump for a private sale. Although the obvious advantage is that there are no agents' fees to pay, you will have to market the property yourself. This means you need to be incredibly organised and always available to conduct viewings. You will need to negotiate a sale price yourself, whereas an agent can act as a mediator on your behalf and justify an asking price. You will undoubtedly have fewer resources, and certainly less experience than the agent to carry out all of these important tasks effectively. And remember, there is a lot of money at stake if you get any of these things wrong.

Personally, I would always sell a property I have spent time, effort and money developing through an agent. Don't be fooled into thinking you will save yourself money on commission fees when there are large sums of cash at stake. There is too much at risk if you can't carry out any of the tasks involved in selling as professionally as an agent. In any case, the chances are pretty high that with all of their marketing skills and resources an agent will get more for your property than you would, which will negate any fee you have to pay them.

# Receiving an offer

Think carefully before accepting an offer. If you receive an offer of less than the full asking price it could be because the buyer does not feel that the property is worth that amount. Alternatively, they may be trying to get a good deal, or perhaps be unable to borrow the full amount.

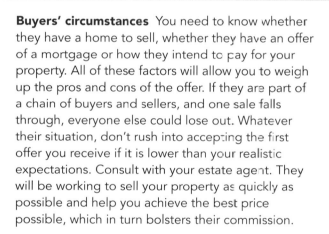

*Generally, don't abandon a vendor in the hope of a quick sale or a bit more money with another buyer – the same flaws are likely to show up on their survey too.*

**Buyers' circumstances** You need to know whether they have a home to sell, whether they have an offer of a mortgage or how they intend to pay for your property. All of these factors will allow you to weigh up the pros and cons of the offer. If they are part of a chain of buyers and sellers, and one sale falls through, everyone else could lose out. Whatever their situation, don't rush into accepting the first offer you receive if it is lower than your realistic expectations. Consult with your estate agent. They will be working to sell your property as quickly as possible and help you achieve the best price possible, which in turn bolsters their commission.

**A reasonable offer** Decide whether to keep the property on the market or to mark it as 'sold subject to contract'. Generally, the offer will be based on you taking it off the market, but if you do want to continue advertising it to invite more offers, then tell the prospective buyer. In England and Wales you can technically accept other offers until the moment you exchange contracts. However, buying and selling property in Scotland and Ireland is different.
　Ask your solicitor to draw up a draft contract. Encourage the purchaser's solicitor via your estate

agent/solicitor to get local authority and other searches requested as soon as possible.

## Valuation and survey

The condition and value of your property is almost certainly going to have to be checked by the buyer. Their mortgage lender will organise a valuation to ensure their investment is safe and the buyer may well arrange for a survey to be carried out.

If the buyer's valuation/survey shows up any problems, your estate agent will advise you on the appropriate course of action to take.

This could involve a number of possible options:
- Lowering your price to continue with the sale.
- Taking the property off the market while you fix the problem and putting it back on the market at a later date.
- Arranging for specialist reports to assess the seriousness of any fault found.

## The deal is done

Almost there! You've done the hard part and it is now time for contracts to be exchanged between both parties' solicitors. Once you have exchanged contracts, you and your buyer are legally committed to one another and at this point the buyer's deposit (normally about 10%) will be paid into your solicitor's account to be held for you until completion.

**Completion**  Finally, the ownership of the property passes from the seller to the buyer. It generally takes place about four weeks after exchange of contracts. The timescale can be longer or it is possible to exchange and complete on the same day.

On completion you will receive from the buyer, via your solicitor, the outstanding balance for the sale of your property, less any fees and your mortgage repayment.

Now is the time for you to take a rest, celebrate or start looking for your next property to develop.

# Selling in Scotland

In Scotland, solicitors not estate agents sell the majority of houses and they will provide a full estate agency service. As well as conveyancing, this will include registering your property in the local solicitors' property centre. The solicitor is likely to charge a percentage fee to cover both the selling and the conveyancing. Get an estimate before going ahead. You can sell via an estate agent but they will normally pass any offers to your solicitor.

The next step is to advertise the property for sale, which your solicitor or estate agent will arrange for you. It is usual to state an asking price (normally the minimum figure you would accept) and invite offers over this sum. Your solicitor will advise you on the asking price and the actual price you should expect.

A prospective buyer's solicitor will contact your solicitor or estate agent to tell them they have an interested party. Unlike in England, parties have to get a survey carried out at this stage, even before an offer has been made.

If several people are interested it is usual to fix a closing date for offers. You are not obliged to accept the highest offer or any of the offers if you do not wish to do so. Once an offer is accepted, both parties' solicitors will liaise to ensure all points of the sale are agreed. These points are then confirmed in writing and this exchange of letters is referred to as the 'missives'. The process takes only a day or two and the conclusion of missives constitutes a binding contract. The short time between offers being made and becoming binding, and the absence of gazumping, are advantages of the Scottish system.

Next your solicitor will finalise the conveyancing. He or she will arrange for the title deeds of the property to be sent to the buyer's solicitor, inform your bank or building society that missives have been concluded and obtain a redemption statement to show the amount of your loan to be repaid on completion of the sale.

# Selling in Ireland (Eire)

The great majority of property in Ireland is sold by private treaty, and it is advisable to use an estate agent to conduct the sale. It is common for agents to also be auctioneers and it is recommended that you choose one who is a member of the Irish Auctioneers and Valuers Institute.

Your agent can suggest a price level on your behalf, although this price is not binding on the seller. Once your property has grabbed the attention of potential buyers, offers will be invited. You would hope to have interest from various parties and to have bid and counter offer at this point. If there is very strong interest in the property, the agent may suggest a closed or private tender. This is essentially a closed competition of final bids from each buyer, with the highest bid winning.

Once you have accepted an offer, it is normal to ask for a deposit; usually this is 5% with a private treaty sale. Your agent should also ensure that your buyer has funds or an approved loan in place. It is normal to cease marketing the property at this stage, although the sale is not secured until a formal contract has been signed and exchanged by you and the buyer. Up until this point you may entertain all offers even though you have already accepted an offer. As in England, gazumping does occur.

It is not uncommon for homes in Ireland to be sold by auction, but you are advised to employ a combined agent/licensed auctioneer if you choose to sell this way. Based on how much interest there is in your property, you and the agent will be able to set your confidential reserve price just before the auction. At the auction, the auctioneers will try to get your price up as far as they can. Once the reserve price has been met, the auctioneer will let the room know and announce that the property is now 'on the market'. The onus is then on all potential buyers to bid competitively for your property. If your house does not meet the reserve price and does not sell, your agent can advise you on continuing negotiations with any bidders who are still interested. In this way you may still make a sale.

Once the hammer has gone down and the property has sold, the auctioneer and buyer sign the contract the agent has prepared on your behalf and the sale is unconditional – the purchaser pays a 10% deposit on the auction day and the balance is normally due 30 days later.

# Selling the lifestyle

Remember that you are not selling your own home and your own style, you are selling to your target market, so don't over-furnish or over-decorate. Do make sure the property is clean, free of clutter and offers prospective buyers a chance for them to see how they can make their own impact on it.

It is at this stage of the project that some developers feel it necessary to accessorise each room. Don't be tempted to do this. If you stuff rooms full of your own idea of lovely trinkets, you can needlessly spend a large amount of money, risk putting off viewers with your taste, and clutter up the newly decorated space. Keep your look clean and uncomplicated. Furthermore, remember with design, less is more. If you have made a good job of your development and it has a beautiful finish, there is no need to overdo it. You should aim to suggest how the viewer could live in the property.

## Furniture

It is never a good idea to buy a lot of furniture to stage a property you are about to sell. You may not be able to re-use the pieces in your next development and will have to pay to put them in storage. You can present a property for sale with furniture from your own home, pieces borrowed from friends and family or hired specifically for the purpose.

Make sure that what you do put into a room suggests how that space can best be used. For example, if you have room for an eating area in a kitchen, add a table and chairs to illustrate the point. If you have a box room, put in a single bed to show that it can hold one. A small bedroom may be able to squeeze in a double bed, so put one in to illustrate that it's a feasible option. You can pick up second-hand bases and mattresses very cheaply. Swathed in crisp white linen they will look as impressive and inviting as if they were brand new.

However, don't let furniture dominate rooms and don't fill them with too much, or add pieces that are too large for the space. Rooms will look smaller and moving around will feel awkward. Arrange furniture to maximise the available space and make sure that colours and styles complement your décor.

## Create a focal point

Use mirrors strategically in the presentation of your property. Placing a mirror in a narrow room will create a sense of depth. In a dark room, it will bounce and reflect light; in a small room, it will increase the sense of space.

If you are short of a great view, cheat by adding a picture or painting from your home or a second-hand shop to create a focal point.

## The finishing touches

Leave bedrooms clean, calm and simple. Dress beds with fresh, crisp linen, preferably white. Keep the kitchen free of clutter – don't be tempted to add china or pots and pans. If you must accessorise, a bowl of fruit, a plant or a bottle of olive oil is enough to add life and colour.

If the bathroom looks too clinical you can always pop in some towels to soften the look. The living room should feel inviting. Some spaces look best bare. If you have a dreary view from a window, invest in a simple blind. Think carefully before spending money on having curtains made, as you really either need to include them in the sale, or risk never using them again. It is better to use fewer pieces of beautiful furniture than lots of tat. Put a table and chairs in a dining area or room – if you do not have a table the right size, get a piece of MDF cut to the optimum size and cover with a simple cloth.

Don't put freshly cut flowers in your property unless you are able to change the water and the flowers at regular intervals. Dead or wilting flowers look and smell terrible. For a low-maintenance alternative, buying plants such as lavender or orchids can work out cheaper than replacing flowers, and they serve the same visual purpose. Use them to add colour and life to your design where you have dead space or need a focal point.

---

## ✓ CHECK**LIST** SELLING

1   *Remember that selling at a profit is your ultimate goal. You will need to be aware of resale prices in your chosen area to calculate your potential profit.*

2   *Present the property to viewers so that they can visualise living in it themselves: simple, uncluttered and with potential.*

3   *Go through the correct procedures for selling and make an educated decision about going through a sole agent or two or more agents.*

4   *Work with your estate agent. Friendly agents are more likely to put their best effort into getting a good deal from you.*

5   *Remember that in other countries the procedure may differ from that in England and Wales.*

# Resources

**Association of Residential Letting Agents**
www.arla.co.uk
0845 345 5752

**Centre for Economics Business Research**
www.cebr.com
020 7324 2850

**Council for Registered Gas Installers (CORGI)**
www.corgi-gas.com
01256 372200

**Council of Mortgage Lenders**
www.cml.org.uk
020 7437 0075

**Department of Trade and Industry (DTI): Guide to fire and safety regulations**
www.dti.gov.uk
020 7215 5000

**Design Council**
www.design-council.org.uk/design
020 7420 5200

**DfES School and College Performance Tables**
www.dfes.gov.uk/performancetables
0845 933 3111

**Electrical Contractors Association Ltd**
www.eca.co.uk
020 7313 4800

**English Heritage**
www.english-heritage.org.uk
0870 333 1181

**Environment Agency**
www.environment-agency.gov.uk
0845 933 3111

**Federation of Master Builders**
www.fmb.org.uk
020 7242 7583

**Gas Consumer's Council**
020 7931 0977

**HM Land Registry**
www.landreg.gov.uk
020 7917 8888

**Homecheck: Property advice website**
www.homecheck.co.uk

**Homesale: Network property website**
www.home-sale.co.uk

**Hometrack: Prices and market trends**
www.hometrack.co.uk

**Independent Financial Advisors Promotion**
www.ifap.org.uk
0800 085 3250

**Inland Revenue**
www.inlandrevenue.gov.uk
0845 605 5999

**Institute of Plumbing**
www.plumbers.org.uk
01708 472791

**Irish Law Society**
www.lawsociety.ie
00 353 1671 0711

**Irish Property News**
www.irishpropertynews.com
00 353 91 565622

**The Leasehold Advisory Sevice: Leasehold valuation tribunals**
www.lease-advice.org.uk
0845 345 1993

**Micropal: Standard &
Poors Investment
Information**
www.funds-sp.com

**National Approved
Letting Scheme**
www.nalscheme.co.uk
01242 581712

**National Association of
Estate Agents**
www.naea.co.uk
01926 496800

**National Association of
Plumbing Heating and
Mechanical Services**
www.aphc.co.uk
0800 542 6060

**National Federation of
Roofing Contractors**
www.nfrc.co.uk
020 7435 0387

**National House
Building Council**
www.nhbc.co.uk
01494 735363

**National Land
Information Services**
www.nlis.org.uk
01279 451625

**National Rail Enquiries**
08457 484950

**Office for Standards
in Education**
www.ofsted.gov.uk
020 7421 6800

**Online Estate Agents**
www.findaproperty.com

**Painting and Decorating
Federation**
020 7608 5093

**Rightmove: Property
advice website**
www.rightmove.co.uk

**Royal Institution of
Chartered Surveyors**
www.rics.org.uk

**Scottish Law Information**
www.scottshlaw.org.uk

**Scottish Law Society**
www.law.scot.org.uk
0131 226 7411

**The Heating Ventilation
Contractors' Association**
www.hvca.org.uk
020 7313 4900

**The Historic Buildings
Bureau for Scotland**
www.historic-scotland.gov.uk
0131 668 8668

**The Law Society**
www.lawsociety.org.uk
020 7242 1222

**The Society of Financial
Advisors**
www.sofa.org.
020 8989 8464

**The Victorian Society**
www.victorian-society.org.uk
020 8994 1019

**Trading Standards Office**
www.tradingstandards.gov.uk

**Up My Street: Local
information website**
www.upmystreet.com

# Index

# Acknowledgements

**For Essential Works**
Editor: Nina Sharman
Designer: Michael Gray
Proof reader and indexer: Dipli Saikia